Bulletproof Android™

Developer's Library Series

Visit **developers-library.com** for a complete list of available products

---

The **Developer's Library Series** from Addison-Wesley provides practicing programmers with unique, high-quality references and tutorials on the latest programming languages and technologies they use in their daily work. All books in the Developer's Library are written by expert technology practitioners who are exceptionally skilled at organizing and presenting information in a way that's useful for other programmers.

Developer's Library books cover a wide range of topics, from open-source programming languages and databases, Linux programming, Microsoft, and Java, to Web development, social networking platforms, Mac/iPhone programming, and Android programming.

Bulletproof Android™

Practical Advice for Building Secure Apps

Godfrey Nolan

✦Addison-Wesley

Upper Saddle River, NJ • Boston • Indianapolis • San Francisco
New York • Toronto • Montreal • London • Munich • Paris • Madrid
Capetown • Sydney • Tokyo • Singapore • Mexico City

Many of the designations used by manufacturers and sellers to distinguish their products are claimed as trademarks. Where those designations appear in this book, and the publisher was aware of a trademark claim, the designations have been printed with initial capital letters or in all capitals.

Android is a trademark of Google.

The author and publisher have taken care in the preparation of this book, but make no expressed or implied warranty of any kind and assume no responsibility for errors or omissions. No liability is assumed for incidental or consequential damages in connection with or arising out of the use of the information or programs contained herein.

For information about buying this title in bulk quantities, or for special sales opportunities (which may include electronic versions; custom cover designs; and content particular to your business, training goals, marketing focus, or branding interests), please contact our corporate sales department at corpsales@pearsoned.com or (800) 382-3419.

For government sales inquiries, please contact governmentsales@pearsoned.com.

For questions about sales outside the United States, please contact international@pearsoned.com.

Visit us on the Web: informit.com/aw

Library of Congress Cataloging-in-Publication Data

Nolan, Godfrey.
  Bulletproof Android : practical advice for building secure apps / Godfrey Nolan.
        pages   cm
  Includes index.
  ISBN 978-0-13-399332-5 (pbk. : alk. paper)
  1. Android (Electronic resource) 2. Application software—Development.
3. Computer security. I. Title.
  QA76.774.A53N654 2014
  005.8—dc23

                                                        2014039900

ISBN-13: 978-0-13-399332-5
ISBN-10: 0-13-399332-9

Text printed in the United States on recycled paper at RR Donnelley in Crawfordsville, Indiana.
First printing, December 2014

Editor-in-Chief
Mark L. Taub

Executive Editor
Laura Lewin

Senior Development Editor
Chris Zahn

Managing Editor
John Fuller

Full-Service Production Manager
Julie B. Nahil

Project Editor
Eclipse Publishing Services

Copy Editor
Diane Freed

Indexer
Jack Lewis

Proofreader
Melissa Panagos

Technical Reviewers
Matt Insko
Dave Truxall

Editorial Assistant
Olivia Basegio

Cover Designer
Chuti Prasertsith

Compositor
Eclipse Publishing Services

❖

This book is dedicated to my son and daughter, Rory and Dayna,
for making me laugh so much over the years.
I'm hoping you too will get to write your own books and plays,
and have the pleasure of one day dedicating them to your own kids.

❖

Contents at a Glance

Contents   ix

Preface   xiii

Acknowledgments   xxi

About the Author   xxiii

1   Android Security Issues   1

2   Protecting Your Code   19

3   Authentication   51

4   Network Communication   87

5   Android Databases   109

6   Web Server Attacks   131

7   Third Party Library Integration   151

8   Device Security   167

9   The Future   179

Index   195

Contents

Preface   xiii

Acknowledgments   xxi

About the Author   xxiii

1 Android Security Issues   1

Why Android?   1

    Decompiling an APK   4

    Art for Art's Sake   7

Guidelines   7

    PCI Mobile Payment Acceptance Security
Guidelines   7

    Google Security   9

    HIPAA Secure   10

    OWASP Top 10 Mobile Risks (2014)   14

    Forrester Research's Top 10 Nontechnical
Security Issues in Mobile App Development   16

Securing the Device   17

    SEAndroid   17

    Federal Information Processing Standard (FIPS)   18

Conclusion   18

2 Protecting Your Code   19

Looking into the classes.dex File   19

Obfuscation Best Practices   24

    No Obfuscation   26

    ProGuard   27

    DexGuard   32

    Security Through Obscurity   38

    Testing   38

Smali   39

    Helloworld   39

    Remove App Store Check   43

Hiding Business Rules in the NDK   48

Conclusion   49

3 Authentication   51

Secure Logins   51

Understanding Best Practices for
User Authentication and Account Validation   54

    Take 1   55

    Take 2   56

    Take 3   59

    Take 4   62

Application Licensing with LVL   65

OAuth   77

    OAuth with Facebook   78

    Web and Mobile Session Management   82

    Vulnerability   84

User Behavior   84

    Two (or More) Factor Authentication   85

Conclusion   86

4 Network Communication   87

HTTP(S) Connection   88

Symmetric Keys   92

Asymmetric Keys   94

Ineffective SSL   99

    Man-in-the-Middle Demo   100

    Root Your Phone   102

    Charles Proxy Test   103

Conclusion   107

5 Android Databases   109

Android Database Security Issues   109

SQLite   110

    Backing Up the Database Using adb   111

    Disabling Backup   115

SQLCipher   116

    Finding the Key   119

Hiding the Key   120

    Ask Each Time   120

    Shared Preferences   122

In the Code   123

In the NDK   124

Web Services   127

SQL Injection   127

Conclusion   129

6 Web Server Attacks   131

Web Services   131

OWASP Web Services Cheat Sheet   133

Replay Attacks   135

Cross Platform   135

WebView Attacks   140

SQL Injection   142

XSS   145

Cloud   146

OWASP Web Top 10 Risks   146

OWASP Cloud Top 10 Risks   148

HIPAA Web Server Compliance   149

Conclusion   150

7 Third-Party Library Integration   151

Transferring the Risk   152

Permissions   152

Installing Third-Party Apps   154

Installing Crittercism   154

Installing Crashlytics   157

Trust but Verify   160

Decompiling SDKs   160

Man in the Middle   163

Conclusion   165

8 Device Security   167

Wiping Your Device   168

Fragmentation   168

adb Backup   169

Logs   169

Device Encryption   172

SEAndroid   174

FIPS 140-2   176

Mobile Device Management   177

Conclusion   178

9 The Future   179

More Sophisticated Attacks   179

Internet of Things   186

   Android Wearables   186

   Ford Sync AppID   187

Audits and Compliance   188

Tools   190

   Drozer   191

   OWASP Mobile Top 10 Risks   193

   Lint   193

Conclusion   194

Index   195

Preface

Why another Android security book? Right now I know of a half dozen books or so about hacking Android. I personally wrote one a few years ago called *Decompiling Android*. In the world of hacking we use the term *white hat* for someone who is trying to improve the security of a system and *black hat* for someone who is trying to exploit the weaknesses of a system. In my opinion, most of the existing Android hacking books are either black hat books or they tread the line between white hat and black hat. Sometimes they benefit a black hat hacker and sometimes the information is useful for someone who wants to write a more secure app. Black hat books are still a great resource for understanding how to secure your app, but the focus is on how to attack rather than how to protect an app.

What This Book Is About

This book is firmly in the white hat category. It is an Android security book for developers, for managers, and for security professionals who want to write more secure Android apps. It uses examples from the many hundreds of Android apps that we (the company I run) have audited over the past three years, and it uses real-world examples of what works and doesn't work from a security perspective. In each chapter we'll look at some examples of how naive coding practices expose apps and how other developers have found more secure solutions.

This book is also written to complement the *Android Security Essentials LiveLessons* video that covers the OWASP (Open Web Application Security Project) Mobile Top 10 Risks in detail. The OWASP Mobile Top 10 is the de facto standard for Android security. And because all security projects are a moving target, the book uses the latest OWASP Mobile Top 10 that has been updated since the LiveLessons video first appeared.

What This Book Is Not About

If you own an Android phone you're probably worried about apps with hidden malware, or what permissions you should or shouldn't accept. We won't be covering those issues as the focus of the book is on Android developers who want to write more secure Android apps, not someone who owns an Android phone. What's more, we're not going to discuss how to root your phone because that really doesn't have much to do with writing secure code. We will touch on its implications for secure apps, but we won't be showing you how to root your phone. From a developer's perspective, that's why you have an emulator.

Why Care?

Over the past two or three years we've downloaded a large number of Android APKs and examined them for any security holes. We've uncovered a wide range of security issues; see Figure P-1 for some examples. These generally fall into the following categories:

1. Keys or API information hard coded in the app (static information)

2. Usernames and passwords and other credentials that are stored insecurely (dynamic information)

3. Sensitive data sent insecurely across the network to a back-end server

4. Third-party libraries collecting and transmitting back to base ad hoc information that they don't need to perform their job

5. Test data or other extraneous information stored in the production APK

It's customary to notify companies that their apps have security issues and are leaking information before releasing the information to the press. This gives the developers some time to fix it and release an update before it goes public. Many times in the past when we contacted the developers responsible for the security issues, we found that security really isn't on their radar as something to worry about. If you're developing mobile apps, then security needs to become part of your development process.

This book comes from what we've seen in our audits of different Android apps. The aim here is to provide you with a book of security anti-patterns where you can see other people's mistakes and hopefully not repeat (m)any of them, thereby keeping your users more secure than your competition.

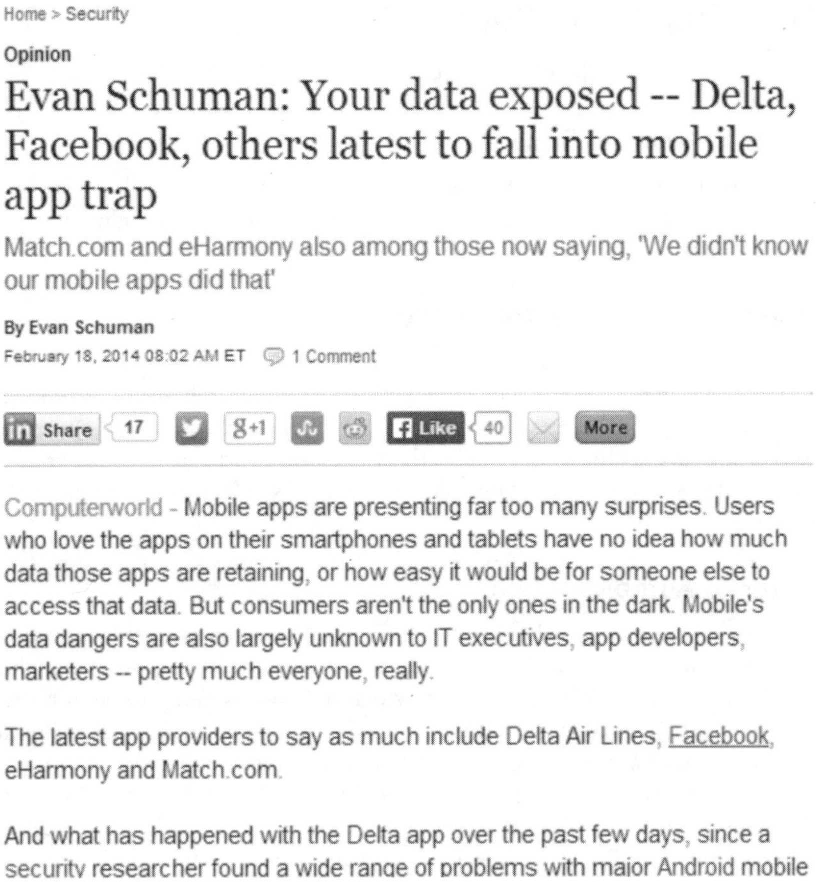

Home > Security

Opinion

Evan Schuman: Your data exposed -- Delta, Facebook, others latest to fall into mobile app trap

Match.com and eHarmony also among those now saying, 'We didn't know our mobile apps did that'

By Evan Schuman
February 18, 2014 08:02 AM ET   💬 1 Comment

Computerworld - Mobile apps are presenting far too many surprises. Users who love the apps on their smartphones and tablets have no idea how much data those apps are retaining, or how easy it would be for someone else to access that data. But consumers aren't the only ones in the dark. Mobile's data dangers are also largely unknown to IT executives, app developers, marketers -- pretty much everyone, really.

The latest app providers to say as much include Delta Air Lines, Facebook, eHarmony and Match.com.

And what has happened with the Delta app over the past few days, since a security researcher found a wide range of problems with major Android mobile

Figure P-1   Dating app insecurity

What This Book Covers

Here is a breakdown of the book by chapter.

Chapter 1: Android Security Issues

Chapter 1 is an introduction to the security issues on the Android platform. We'll show how to decompile an Android APK and look at some of the industry standard guidelines for securing the Android platform.

Chapter 2: Protecting Your Code

In Chapter 2, we'll look at how to download and reverse engineer an Android APK back into Java source in more detail. We'll also cover how to best protect your code using different types of obfuscation tools and techniques that we've encountered during our audits. We'll look at the implications of being able to disassemble your code into bytecode. And we'll show how you can use the NDK to hide your algorithms and business rules.

Chapter 3: Authentication

Providing a secure login mechanism for your mobile users is harder than on the Web. The trend with mobile devices is to make things as easy as possible for the user. Mobile keyboards are small, so it's unlikely that someone is going to enter more than six characters to log in to an app. But if you make it too easy to log in to your app, then you run the risk of unauthorized users gaining access to sensitive data by going around your authentication. In Chapter 3 we'll look at how some of the authentication mechanisms in our audits have failed, and we're also going to look at what developers have been using to log in to mobile apps that have been a lot more effective.

Chapter 4: Network Communication

In modern browsers, if you connect via secure HTTP, or HTTPS over a secure sockets layer, you'll get a little green lock, or a gold one depending on your browser, to indicate that you're in a secure encrypted transaction. Developers pay a Certificate Authority (CA) to make sure that they are who they say they are. And if you happen to come across a site that isn't a valid site, your web browser will alert you pretty quickly that something is wrong. Unfortunately, there isn't anything similar in mobile computing—there is no lock or key to comfort the user that any network communication is encrypted.

In this chapter we'll first take a look at how to send information securely across the network using SSL. In the second part of the chapter we'll look at how hackers might perform a man-in-the-middle attack using an SSL Proxy that intercepts the communication and sees whether it's really secure.

Chapter 5: Android Databases

One of the most basic questions about Android security and mobile security in general is, "What information should you store on a device, and where can you store it securely?" Ideally, you would not store or cache anything on the device. But if someone doesn't have any mobile service—for example, when on an airplane without wi-fi—then you're going to cause some frustration if this person can't log into the app for a number of hours. In this chapter we'll talk about where you can store data and how using the wrong permissions can allow other apps to read your data. Finally, we'll explain how to write data securely to an SD card as well as a SQLite database.

Chapter 6: Web Server Attacks

Most mobile apps that do real work will in some way connect to a back-end web server. If the communication is via a web service, this can either be via SOAP or, more commonly, by using a REST web service. In this chapter it's a case of what's old is new again. We'll explore how the same security best practices that have applied to web servers for the past 20 years apply to web servers used in mobile apps. We'll also look at how we can use logins from other website break-ins to help secure our authentication.

Chapter 7: Third-Party Library Integration

Data leakage from third-party apps is perhaps a less obvious way that someone can recover a user's information from your app. In this chapter we'll explain the meaning behind side channel data leakage and learn how to track what information is being passed by your app to other services, with or without your knowledge.

Chapter 8: Device Security

Running your APK on different versions of Android can have different security problems. In this chapter we'll look at how Android device fragmentation needs to be considered when you're writing a secure app. Different environments have different requirements: Corporations have different requirements than individuals, health care needs HIPAA compliance, and government work probably means that your Android phone needs to be FIPS compliant. In this chapter we'll also look at how Samsung Knox and SELinux or SEAndroid are being used to make your device more secure.

Chapter 9: The Future

There aren't many certainties about where Android security is going. But in Chapter 9 we're going to look into the crystal ball: Using Android L as well as some open source ideas, we'll do our best to predict what future versions of Android will provide from a security perspective. This way, you'll know what existing security challenges will be solved and what new challenges lie ahead. We'll also look at how Android attacks are likely to get more sophisticated in the near future.

Tools

There are lots of tools that we'll be using again and again throughout this book. Most of them are listed here for convenience.

- 010, a hex editor that includes a template for disassembling classes.dex files. 010 does a great job of parsing the classes.dex file (see Figure P-2). It can be found at www.sweetscape.com/010editor/.

- Abe, the Android Backup Extractor. It is used to convert an Android backup into a tar format so that it can be unzipped. It's available from https://github.com/nelenkov/android-backup-extractor.

- adb, the Android debug bridge. It comes as part of the Android SDK.

- apktool, a collection of tools. It includes Smali and Baksmali as well as AXMLPrinter2.

- AXMLPrinter2, which converts the compressed AndroidManifest.xml in an APK back into a readable format. It's available at https://code.google.com/p/android4me/downloads/list.

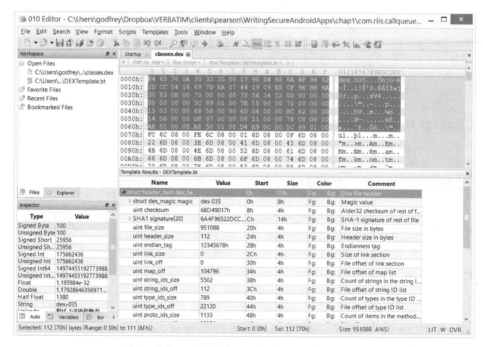

Figure P-2   010 Editor parsing classes.dex file

- Baksmali and Smali, the Android disassembler and assembler. You can find them at https://code.google.com/p/smali/ or as part of apk-tool.

- Charles Proxy, a tool for testing for man-in-the-middle attacks. It's available from http://www.charlesproxy.com/.

- Dedexer, a classes.dex dump file. Written by Gabor Paller in Hungary, it's available from http://dedexer.sourceforge.net/.

- dex2jar, which converts APKs to Java jar files for decompilation. You can find it at https://code.google.com/p/dex2jar/.

- Drozer, an attack tool for Android apps. It's available from https://www.mwrinfosecurity.com/products/drozer/.

- JD-GUI, one of many Java decompilers. You can find it at http://jd.benow.ca/.

- Jadx, one of a new breed of Android decompilers. It's available at https://github.com/skylot/jadx.

- Keyczar, which we use for our public/private key encryption. You can download it from http://keyczar.org.

- Lint, which comes with the Android SDK.

- ProGuard and DexGuard, which are obfuscators. ProGuard ships with the Android SDK, and DexGuard is available at www.saikoa.com/.

- sqlitebrowser, a GUI for SQLite databases. It's available from http://sqlitebrowser.org/.

Acknowledgments

Laura Lewin—I lost count of the number of times Laura hounded me on items that were due or, more often than not, overdue. I sincerely appreciate your patience.

David Truxall and Matt Insko—Thanks to my two technical reviewers. I've worked with good reviewers and bad reviewers in the past. The better ones try the code, make suggestions for things you missed, and help get you to the finish line without losing your mind. Dave and Matt are the best.

Cameron Beyer and Paul Moon—Thanks for your help with the coding, especially when I wasn't very specific about what I was trying to do. ☺

Chris Zahn—Thanks for the editing. Your quality and speed are amazing.

About the Author

Godfrey Nolan is founder and president of the mobile and web development company RIIS LLC based in Troy, Michigan, and Belfast, Northern Ireland. This is his fourth book. He has had a healthy obsession with reverse engineering bytecode since he wrote "Decompile Once, Run Anywhere," which first appeared in *Web Techniques* magazine way back in September 1997. Godfrey is originally from Dublin, Ireland.

Android Security Issues

Chapter 1 provides an introduction to the security issues on the Android platform. We show you how to decompile an Android APK and look at some of the industry standard guidelines for securing the Android platform.

Why Android?

Android runs on what is called a virtual machine (VM), specifically known as the Dalvik Virtual Machine (DVM), which runs within the entire Android framework (see Figure 1-1). VMs are designed so that the code is interpreted instruction by instruction at runtime rather than compiled into a binary format to be executed at a later stage.

In an iOS binary everything is known at compile time. The phone chip, type of phone, and version of iOS are all known when the developer readies his or her app for the iTunes app store. In this way, only the minimum amount of instructions and data is stored in the file that gets downloaded to your phone from iTunes.

> **Note**
>
> It's not just Android APKs that are interpreted. Visual Basic, .Net, and Java—as just a few examples—use this virtual machine concept.

The beauty of a VM is that it can run on lots of different chips and devices, and as long as the device designers follow the DVM spec your APK should run on it without any changes. It's not surprising that Android uses this VM architecture, as there are now tens of thousands of different devices that all need to be able to support the same DVM. Android code is only compiled when you run the app on your phone, so by its very design there will be much more information in an APK than in a similar iOS binary. Furthermore, the data and instructions are also going to be separated out,

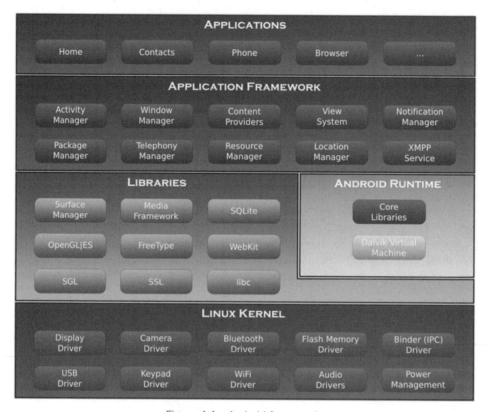

Figure 1-1   Android framework

making it much easier to reverse engineer the code back into something close to its original format.

Hackers use a tool called a decompiler to convert VM code back into original source. Many Java decompilers are available, and because of Android's relationship to Java, any Android code compiled from Java code is open to decompilation.

When you build an Android app in Eclipse or Android Studio, it is first compiled in Java. Then a tool called "dx," which comes with the Android SDK, converts the Java jar file into a classes.dex file (see the Android build process in Figure 1-2). Decompiling an Android APK is a two-stage process: The .dex file is first converted back into .class files using a tool called dex2jar where it can then be decompiled using your favorite Java decompiler, such as JD-GUI.

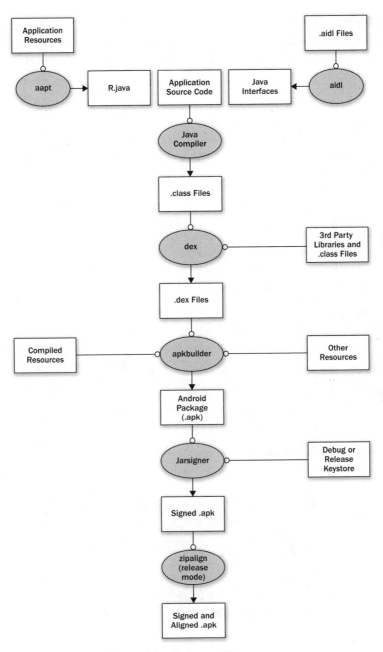

Figure 1-2   Android build process

Decompiling an APK

The first step in decompiling an APK is to get ahold of one. There are a number of ways to do this, but I prefer to use the adb command (Android debug bridge) tool that comes with the Android Developer Kit as part of the Android SDK. The adb command allows you to pull a copy of the APK off the phone onto your PC for further analysis.

To download an APK onto to your PC from your phone, connect your phone to your PC using your USB phone cable and then turn on the USB debugging under the developer options on your Android phone. Next, you need to know the name of the APK that you want. You don't need to root the phone if you're running anything below Android 4.3 to pull an APK off the phone because the naming convention and location follow the same basic rules.

We can get the name by searching for the ID in Google Play. In this example, we're looking for the Call Queue Manager APK, which we'll assume has already been installed on your Android phone. Now search for the app on Google Play and copy the ID in the Google Play URL (see Figure 1-3). We'll use this to get the APK onto our PC.

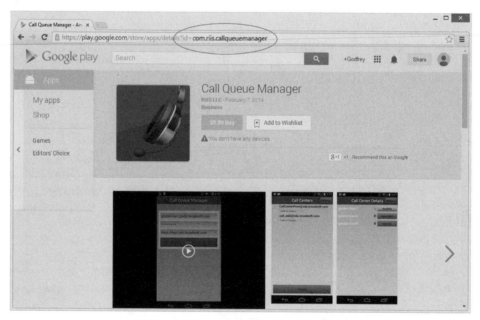

Figure 1-3   Find the ID in Google Play.

The APK is in the /data/app folder and will be called whatever the ID is in the querystring of the URL in Figure 1-3 with a -1.apk appended.

Now that we've found the APK, we can pull it onto the PC on most Android phones by typing the command

```
adb pull /data/app/com.riis.callqueuemanager-1.apk
```

Dex2jar is a tool for converting Android .dex format to Java's .class format—just one binary format to another binary format—but not to the Java source. You still have to run a Java decompiler on the resulting jar file to view the source.

Dex2jar is available on Google code and was written by Pan Xiaobo, a graduate student at Zhejiang University in China.

If we unzip the Call Queue Manager APK file (see Figure 1-4), we can see some files and folders familiar to any Android developer, such as assets and resources folders, and the AndroidManifest file. The classes.dex file contains all the programming instructions needed to run your Android app.

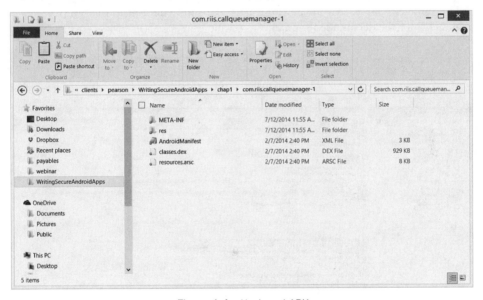

Figure 1-4   Unzipped APK

Currently, what makes Android decompilation possible is its relationship to Java. The Java files you write in Eclipse or Android Studio are first compiled into Java class files and then further compiled into a classes.dex file before being added to the APK.

Dex2jar can revert classes.dex back into a Java jar file, which can then be decompiled with your favorite decompiler, such as JD-GUI. Executing the dex2jar file against the apk file from the command line will convert it into a Java jar file.

```
dex2jar com.riis.callqueuemanager-1.apk
```

There are more than a dozen Java decompilers available, but JD-GUI is the de facto Java decompiler. It was written by Emmanuel Dupuy from Paris and is available for free from the website http://jd.benow.ca/.

Java decompilers work because, unlike compiled code, all virtual machines interpret the binary. Therefore, more data and instructions are in a Java jar file, allowing people to reverse engineer these binary files into something approaching the original code, albeit without any comments. To decompile our Call Queue Manager file, simply drag and drop the jar file that you just converted using dex2jar into JD-GUI to reveal the decompiled source, or you can run it from the command line as follows (see Figure 1-5 for the decompiled source):

```
jd-gui com.riis.callqueuemanager-1 _ dex2jar.jar
```

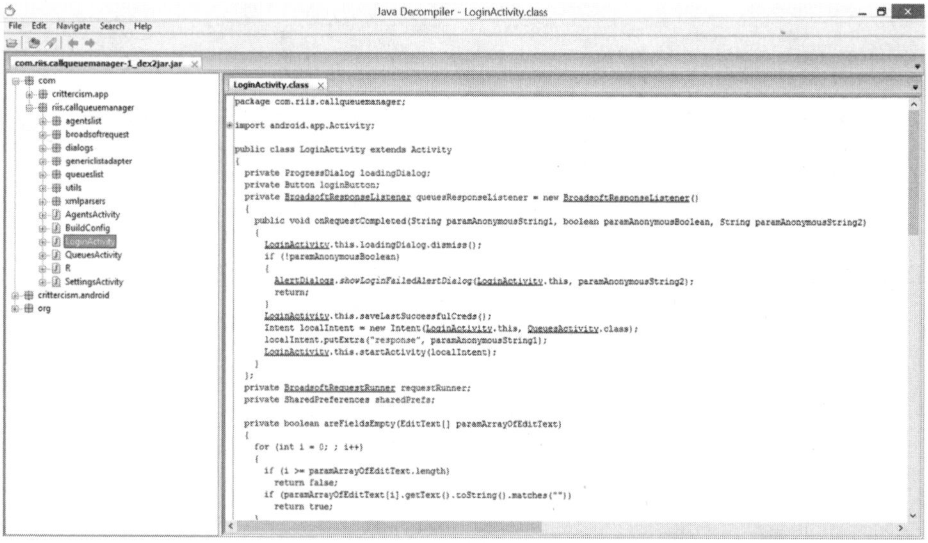

Figure 1-5   JD-GUI

Art for Art's Sake

Earlier we said that the DVM interprets the bytecode, but we weren't being 100 percent accurate. The DVM uses a Just in Time (JIT) compiler rather than a simple interpreter, which has the benefit of many years of the JVM compiler theory and thus gives much better performance than a basic interpreter. JIT compilers are a lot faster than straightforward interpreters. JIT doesn't have any effect either way on security because the classes.dex is not modified by the compiler.

In KitKat, Google introduced a new VM called the Android Runtime (ART). This new type of VM, called an Ahead-Of-Time (AOT) compiler, optimizes the classes.dex file when it is installed on the phone or device. Currently you can use either the DVM or ART on your KitKat-enabled phone. However, Google announced at Google I/O 2014 that ART will be the only VM in Android 4.5 and above. Right now, and for the foreseeable future, ART also has no effect on decompilation, as we can still access the unoptimized APK before it hits ART. The structure of an ART classes.dex in Android 4.4 is still the same format as the DVM classes.dex until it gets AOT compiled, and even then it is not significantly different.

Guidelines

It's not surprising that Android developers get confused as to the best approach to use from a security perspective. There are so many security lists out there it's hard to know which items are the most important.

Here are the main lists that we're going to look at:

- PCI Mobile Payment Acceptance Security Guidelines
- Google Security
- HIPAA Secure
- OWASP Top 10 Mobile Risk (2014)
- Forrester Research's Top 10 Nontechnical Security Issues in Mobile App Development

Each has its own merits, but the one that stands out is the OWASP Top 10. However, let's briefly review each of them.

PCI Mobile Payment Acceptance Security Guidelines

PCI is the Payment Card Industry Security Standards Council, the group responsible for the security of payments online or otherwise, which was set up by the credit card industry in 2006. The focus of this list is, not surprisingly, on the safety of credit card payments on mobile devices. Nothing is Android specific and could just as well apply to iOS or Windows phones.

It's important to note that PCI's Mobile Payment Acceptance Security Guidelines are guidelines and as yet are not mandatory, so if you fail to meet these guidelines there are no obvious fines. The list, published in September 2012, is as follows:

1. Prevent account data from being intercepted when entered into a mobile device.
2. Prevent account data from being compromised while processed or stored within the mobile device.
3. Prevent account data from interception upon transmission out of the mobile device.
4. Prevent unauthorized logical-device access.
5. Create server-side controls and report unauthorized access.
6. Prevent escalation of privileges.
7. Create the ability to remotely disable payment application.
8. Detect theft or loss.
9. Harden supporting systems.
10. Prefer online transactions.
11. Conform to secure coding, engineering, and testing.
12. Protect against known vulnerabilities.
13. Protect the mobile device from unauthorized applications.
14. Protect the mobile device from malware.
15. Protect the mobile device from unauthorized attachments.
16. Create instructional materials for implementation and use.
17. Support secure merchant receipts.
18. Provide an indication of a secure state.

The key points in this list are to make sure you encrypt credit card data when it's entered on the device and also when it's being transmitted to the server.

The complete report can be downloaded from https://www.pcisecuritystandards.org /documents/Mobile_Payment_Security_Guidelines_Developers_v1.pdf.

Google Security

Google doesn't provide a top ten list as such, but does have a Security Best Practices training resource, listed below. Unlike the previous list, this one is specific to Android, which is no surprise as it comes from Google.

1. Avoid opening the files MODE_WORLD_WRITEABLE or MODE_WORLD_READABLE because other apps can read them.

2. Do not store sensitive information using external storage because someone can view the data on the SD card without any protection.

3. If you do not intend to provide other applications with access to your ContentProvider, mark them as android:exported=false in the application manifest.

4. Minimize the number of permissions that your app requests; don't ask for what you don't need.

5. Use HTTPS over HTTP anywhere that HTTPS is supported on the server.

6. Use Google Cloud Messaging (GCM) and IP networking for sending data messages from a web server to your app on a user device.

7. Use SQL parameterized queries to protect against SQL injection.

8. If you can avoid storing or transmitting the information, do not store or transmit the data.

9. To prevent XSS attacks, do not directly use JavaScript within a WebView and do not call setJavaScriptEnabled().

10. Use existing cryptographic algorithms, don't invent your own, and use a secure random number generator, SecureRandom, to initialize any cryptographic keys.

11. If you need to store a key for repeated use, use a mechanism like KeyStore that provides a mechanism for long-term storage and retrieval of cryptographic keys.

12. If data within a broadcast intent may be sensitive, you should consider applying a permission to make sure that malicious applications cannot register to receive those messages without appropriate permissions.

13. Binder or Messenger is the preferred mechanism for RPC-style IPC in Android.

14. Don't load code from outside of your application APK.

15. Avoid native code because of buffer overflow concerns.

Currently, some of the items, such as opening a file in MODE_WORLD_
READABLE, are actually quite hard to do without Eclipse or the Android Studio
complaining. All of these and more are covered when you use lint on your Android
project. We'll be looking at these in a lot more detail throughout the book.

This list is available from http://developer.android.com/training/articles
/security-tips.html.

HIPAA Secure

The impacts of mobile security in the healthcare space are covered in the United States
by HIPAA, which stands for the Health Insurance Portability and Accountability Act.
Other countries have similar rules. Being HIPAA secure means that you are not leaking any protected health information (PHI). Be warned that HIPAA has not caught
up with the rapid developments in the mobile world. However, using some common
sense, the same principals apply, with some exceptions given that the computer is no
longer tied to a desk inside an office.

HealthIT.gov provides a Security Risk Assessment Tool, which is a good place
to start to determine whether your app is HIPAA compliant. It's available at
www.healthit.gov/providers-professionals/security-risk-assessment-tool and is split
into three areas: Administrative, Technical, and Physical Safeguards. The technical
safeguards, T1 to T45, are listed in Table 1-1, with some of the more interesting rules
from an Android perspective shown in bold. The safeguards are termed as Standard,
Required, and Addressable. Standard and Required should all be implemented. There
is some debate as to whether all Addressables need to be completed or not, as the
HIPAA documentation talks about how they are analogous to "Alternatives." However, if they apply to your situation they should be implemented.

Table 1-1 **SRA Risk Assessment Tool—Technical Section**

Number	Type	Safeguard
T1	Standard	Does your practice have policies and procedures requiring safeguards to limit access to ePHI to those persons and software programs appropriate for their role?
T2	Standard	Does your practice have policies and procedures to grant access to ePHI based on the person or software programs appropriate for their role?
T3	**Standard**	**Does your practice analyze the activities performed by all of its workforce and service providers to identify the extent to which each needs access to ePHI?**
T4	Standard	Does your practice identify the security settings for each of its information systems and electronic devices that control access?
T5	**Required**	**Does your practice have policies and procedures for the assignment of a unique identifier for each authorized user?**
T6	Required	Does your practice require that each user enter a unique user identifier prior to obtaining access to ePHI?
T7	**Required**	**Does your practice have policies and procedures to enable access to ePHI in the event of an emergency?**
T8	Required	Does your practice define what constitutes an emergency and identify the various types of emergencies that are likely to occur?
T9	Required	Does your practice have policies and procedures for creating an exact copy of ePHI as a backup?
T10	**Required**	**Does your practice back up ePHI by saving an exact copy to a magnetic disk/tape or a virtual storage, such as a cloud environment?**
T11	Required	Does your practice have backup information systems so that it can access ePHI in the event of an emergency or when your practice's primary systems become unavailable?
T12	Required	Does your practice have the capability to activate emergency access to its information systems in the event of a disaster?
T13	Required	Does your practice have policies and procedures to identify the role of the individual accountable for activating emergency access settings when necessary?
T14	Required	Does your practice designate a workforce member who can activate the emergency access settings for your information systems?
T15	Required	Does your practice test access when evaluating its ability to continue accessing ePHI and other health records during an emergency?

Continues

Table 1-1 **SRA Risk Assessment Tool—Technical Section (*Continued*)**

Number	Type	Safeguard
T16	Required	Does your practice effectively recover from an emergency and resume normal operations and access to ePHI?
T17	**Addressable**	**Does your practice have policies and procedures that require an authorized user's session to be automatically logged-off after a predetermined period of inactivity?**
T18	Addressable	Does a responsible person in your practice know the automatic logoff settings for its information systems and electronic devices?
T19	Addressable	Does your practice activate an automatic logoff that terminates an electronic session after a predetermined period of user inactivity?
T20	Addressable	Does your practice have policies and procedures for implementing mechanisms that can encrypt and decrypt ePHI?
T21	Addressable	Does your practice know the encryption capabilities of its information systems and electronic devices?
T22	Addressable	Does your practice control access to ePHI and other health information by using encryption/decryption methods to deny access to unauthorized users?
T23	**Standard**	**Does your practice have policies and procedures identifying hardware, software, or procedural mechanisms that record or examine information systems activities?**
T24	Standard	Does your practice identify its activities that create, store, and transmit ePHI and the information systems that support these business processes?
T25	Standard	Does your practice categorize its activities and information systems that create, transmit, or store ePHI as high, moderate, or low risk based on its risk analyses?
T26	Standard	Does your practice use the evaluation from its risk analysis to help determine the frequency and scope of its audits when identifying the activities that will be tracked?
T27	Standard	Does your practice have audit control mechanisms that can monitor, record, and/or examine information system activity?
T28	Standard	Does your practice have policies and procedures for creating, retaining, and distributing audit reports to appropriate workforce members for review?
T29	**Standard**	**Does your practice generate the audit reports and distribute them to the appropriate people for review?**

Table 1-1 **SRA Risk Assessment Tool—Technical Section**

Number	Type	Safeguard
T30	Standard	Does your practice have policies and procedures establishing retention requirements for audit purposes?
T31	Standard	Does your practice retain copies of its audit/access records?
T32	Standard	Does your practice have policies and procedures for protecting ePHI from unauthorized modification or destruction?
T33	Addressable	Does your practice have mechanisms to corroborate that ePHI has not been altered, modified, or destroyed in an unauthorized manner?
T34	Required	Does your practice have policies and procedures for verification that a person or entity seeking access to ePHI is the one claimed?
T35	Required	Does your practice know the authentication capabilities of its information systems and electronic devices to assure that a uniquely identified user is the one claimed?
T36	Required	Does your practice use the evaluation from its risk analysis to select the appropriate authentication mechanism?
T37	Required	Does your practice protect the confidentiality of the documentation containing access control records (list of authorized users and passwords)?
T38	Standard	Does your practice have policies and procedures for guarding against unauthorized access of ePHI when it is transmitted on an electronic network?
T39	**Standard**	**Does your practice implement safeguards to assure that ePHI is not accessed while en route to its intended recipient?**
T40	Addressable	Does your practice know what encryption capabilities are available to it for encrypting ePHI being transmitted from one point to another?
T41	**Addressable**	**Does your practice take steps to reduce the risk that ePHI can be intercepted or modified when it is being sent electronically?**
T42	**Addressable**	**Does your practice implement encryption as the safeguard to assure that ePHI is not compromised when being transmitted from one point to another?**
T44	**Addressable**	**Does your practice have policies and procedures for encrypting ePHI when deemed reasonable and appropriate?**
T45	**Addressable**	**When analyzing risk, does your practice consider the value of encryption for assuring that the integrity of ePHI is not accessed or modified when it is stored or transmitted?**

By substituting the term *mobile app* for *practice* we can see that the same basic rules of securely storing and transmitting PHI data apply. But you also need to think about policies and processes in a lot more detail if something goes wrong and you need to be able to audit your data access so that you can determine whether and when someone gained access to PHI data that was not secured. Security is not just about making the app secure; it's also about what you have in place to notify people if an app has been compromised and being able to find out just what has been compromised so it can be reported. Most mobile development isn't even contemplating mobile security on this level, and it currently includes little or no monitoring of how users are accessing an app's information.

The SRA Tool is a valuable resource that contains a lot more information than can be covered in a single table.

We'll be covering HIPAA in detail throughout the book.

OWASP Top 10 Mobile Risks (2014)

The 2014 OWASP Top 10 is shown below, with further explanations in the paragraphs that follow.

- M1: Weak Server-Side Controls
- M2: Insecure Data Storage
- M3: Insufficient Transport Layer Protection
- M4: Unintended Data Leakage
- M5: Poor Authorization and Authentication
- M6: Broken Cryptography
- M7: Client-Side Injection
- M8: Security Decisions via Untrusted Inputs
- M9: Improper Session Handling
- M10: Lack of Binary Protections

The OWASP Top 10 Mobile Risks list was recently updated to remove some duplication and make it less confusing.

M1: Weak Server-Side Controls

Most mobile apps that do real work will in some way connect to a back-end web server. If the communication is via a web service, then this can be either via SOAP or, more commonly, using a REST web service. The same security best practices that apply to web servers for the past 20 years apply to web servers used in mobile apps.

M2: Insecure Data Storage

Probably the most common area for security problems is where Android developers leave insecure usernames, passwords, IDs, keys, databases, and so forth—in the shared preferences and database folders.

M3: Insufficient Transport Layer Protection

All sensitive information transmitted across the Internet should be done using a secure connection. Does your application use SSL with signed SSL certificates that can't be read using an SSL Proxy tool?

M4: Unintended Data Leakage

This involves sending a user's unauthorized personal information to a third party. This can occur when you're sending data to the event log or in a file that can be read from another app. It can also be caused by a third-party Ad library that's collecting location (or other) information and sending it back to another database without you knowing.

M5: Poor Authorization and Authentication

If the app allows the user to create an account, then the password should contain four or more characters. Four-digit pins are not very secure, so does it check for brute force attacks? If the app is available offline, where is the password stored? And can someone find it on the Android file system?

M6: Broken Cryptography

See if the key is stored in the source code or on a local database where it can be used to unencrypt stored passwords or other data.

M7: Client-Side Injection

Hybrid or cross-platform apps can be compromised using SQL injection attacks. Make sure SQL injection does not work on username and password fields, and so forth.

M8: Security Decisions via Untrusted Inputs

Developers trust too much, but others may abuse that trust, so we need to know how to not fall into that trap. Look for evidence of insecure data input from other applications and sources. Android intents are used to send information between apps, and someone can use intents to bypass Android permissions in IPC or inter-process communication.

M9: Improper Session Handling

User login sessions are often not terminated upon closing the application. This allows users to remain logged in to their account on the application once the app is closed, with the app resuming and making their credit card or other information available next time someone starts the app on the tablet.

M10: Lack of Binary Protections

Obfuscate your code so it can't be completely reverse engineered back into the original source code. Unfortunately, obfuscation is not a silver bullet. Use obfuscators to make it cumbersome for hackers to break your app, but don't obfuscate thinking nobody will be able to decompile your APK.

Forrester Research's Top 10 Nontechnical Security Issues in Mobile App Development

Tyler Shields of Forrester Research brought out a very different nontechnical Top 10 list of mobile security risks, but it's just as appropriate as the previous lists. This Top 10 does a great job of explaining the current state of security when it comes to mobile development.

1. Inadequate developer incentives

2. Lack of mobile-specific security education

3. Inadequate resources available for mobile development security

4. Security without consideration for human factors

5. Taking security out of the hands of the developer

6. Ignorance of the business need

7. Securing mobile, which means securing Agile

8. Focusing on security while ignoring privacy

9. Lack of security in design, development, and QA

10. Security as a bolt-on: post-production security

The following list provides brief explanations of each Top Ten item.

1. **Inadequate developer incentives**. Developers are not properly incentivized to write secure code

2. **Lack of mobile-specific security education**. Developers do not understand the nuances between mobile and general application architectures and security.

3. **Inadequate resources available for mobile development security**. Mobile development security is under-resourced and overburdened, making insecurity a foregone conclusion.

4. **Security without consideration for human factors**. The human factors around security in mobility are very different from nonmobile. Security without consideration of human factors will result in suboptimal security decisions and controls.

5. **Taking security out of the hands of the developer**. Improve the security of tools and frameworks, but don't rely solely on tools to enforce a good secure coding methodology.

6. **Ignorance of the business need**. Developers must understand the business need of the products they are creating. Creation in a vacuum leads to poor business solutions.

7. **Securing mobile, which means securing Agile**. Mobile has changed the face of development. Shorter development cycles and smaller teams are making enterprise development teams rethink their processes.

8. **Focusing on security while ignoring privacy**. Security and privacy are inseparably intertwined. If you ignore one, expect the other to suffer as well.

9. **Lack of security in design, development, and QA**. The concept of a secure development lifecycle has been around for ages. It still applies even with the modified cycles we see in mobile development. Improve your SDLC to lower your flaw count.

10. **Security as a bolt-on: post-production security**. As a post-production security tool, application wrapping and application hardening can help raise the bar of security for your released products. It doesn't hurt to apply another security layer to your applications.

Securing the Device

In certain circumstances you have more control over what types of devices have access to your app. An APK does not necessarily have to be published on an app store. It can be distributed with a corporation or enterprise and never see Google Play. Certain devices can also be encrypted and make it a lot harder for someone to gain access to the data and files even if they have physical access to the device.

SEAndroid

Security Enhanced Linux, or SELinux, was created by the NSA and Red Hat to provide a secure Linux OS. Because Android is yet another flavor of Linux, it is no surprise that SELinux would morph or branch out into Security Enhanced Android, or SEAndroid. This enhances the Android system by adding SELinux support to the kernel and user space. While SEAndroid was installed in Android 4.3 it was in permissive mode, meaning that if any security errors were caught they were simply ignored. SEAndroid on Android 4.4, or KitKat, is now in enforced mode.

Federal Information Processing Standard (FIPS)

Federal agencies demand that your computer equipment is FIPS 140-2 compliant before you can do business securely with the government. To quote from the government's National Institute of Standards and Technology (NIST) website:

> The FIPS 140-2 standard is applicable to all Federal agencies that use cryptographic-based security systems to protect sensitive information in computer and telecommunication systems (including voice systems) as defined in Section 5131 of the Information Technology Management Reform Act of 1996, Public Law 104-106.

A good list of all the FIPS-2 compliant devices and software can be found at http://csrc.nist.gov/groups/STM/cmvp/documents/140-1/140val-all.htm.

Many of the Samsung devices, such as the S4, S5, and Note 3, are FIPS 140-2 compliant using Samsung's Knox environment.

Conclusion

In this chapter we got started with our foray into Android security. We explored some aspects of Android technology and took a look at some of the industry standard security lists as well as dipped into device security. From the lists it should be clear that the golden rules of Android security that are emerging are: (1) Don't store anything on the phone that you don't have to, and (2) transmit the data securely over SSL.

Protecting Your Code

For many developers, protecting your code means enabling ProGuard and then forgetting about it. In this chapter we cover why you need ProGuard in the first place and what it does under the covers. We also look at some other less commonly used tools and techniques that protect your code and why you may want to explore other options.

From the first chapter we know how the architecture of the DVM allows someone to decompile an APK back into Java. In this chapter we're first going to look at the structure of the classes.dex file to show where the bytecodes can be found. Bytecodes are the low-level instructions that your Java code gets converted into so that they can run on the DVM. And bytecodes are made up of two parts: opcode or instruction followed by one or more parameters.

Looking into the classes.dex File

The structure of the classes.dex file is published by Google. You can find the complete specification at https://source.android.com/devices/tech/dalvik/dex-format.html. You can see a simple schematic of the file format in Figure 2-1.

An excellent way to do your own deep dive into the classes.dex format is to use some sort of classes.dex viewer such as the one provided by the 010 Editor. You'll need to follow these steps:

1. Unzip an APK by renaming the extension to zip and then unzipping. If you can't find one, check the online source code for this chapter.

2. Open classes.dex using the 010 Editor.

3. Download the classes.dex template, DEXTemplate.bt, from www.sweetscape.com/010editor/templates/.

4. Hit F5 to run the template.

5. The classes.dex header is highlighted in Figure 2-2. You can see the values for the header as well as where it lives in the classes.dex file.

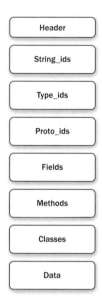

Figure 2-1   Format of a classes.dex file

```
classes.dex
Edit As: Hex     Run Script     Run Template: DEXTemplate.bt

         0  1  2  3  4  5  6  7  8  9  A  B  C  D  E  F   0123456789ABCDEF
0000h:  64 65 78 0A 30 33 35 00 17 90 D4 68 6A 4F 96 52  dex.035...ÔhjO-R
0010h:  2D CC 04 16 69 7D 8A 27 44 19 C9 E5 CF 9E BB 6A  -Ì..i}Š'D.ÉåÏž»j
0020h:  30 83 0E 00 70 00 00 00 78 56 34 12 00 00 00 00  0ƒ..p...xV4.....
0030h:  00 00 00 00 5C 99 01 00 7E 15 00 00 70 00 00 00  ....\™..~...p...
0040h:  15 03 00 00 68 56 00 00 6D 04 00 00 BC 62 00 00  ....hV..m...¼b..
0050h:  14 06 00 00 D8 97 00 00 06 11 00 00 78 C8 00 00  ....Ø-....xÈ..
0060h:  AB 01 00 00 A8 50 01 00 D4 E9 0C 00 5C 99 01 00  «...¨P..Ôé..\™.
0070h:  FC 6C 08 00 FE 6C 08 00 01 6D 08 00 0F 6D 08 00  ül..þl...m...m..
0080h:  22 6D 08 00 3E 6D 08 00 41 6D 08 00 45 6D 08 00  "m..>m..Am..Em..
0090h:  4B 6D 08 00 4E 6D 08 00 52 6D 08 00 61 6D 08 00  Km..Nm..Rm..am..
00A0h:  66 6D 08 00 6B 6D 08 00 6F 6D 08 00 74 6D 08 00  fm..km..om..tm..
00B0h:  79 6D 08 00 7E 6D 08 00 83 6D 08 00 88 6D 08 00  ym..~m..fm..^m..
00C0h:  8D 6D 08 00 98 6D 08 00 9E 6D 08 00 A6 6D 08 00  .m..~m..žm..¦m..
00D0h:  BB 6D 08 00 CC 6D 08 00 D5 6D 08 00 E6 6D 08 00  »m..Ìm..Õm..æm..
00E0h:  EC 6D 08 00 04 6E 08 00 19 6E 08 00 4E 6E 08 00  ìm...n...n..Nn..
```

Template Results - DEXTemplate.bt

Name	Value	Start	Size	Color		Comment
struct header_item dex_header		0h	70h	Fg:	Bg:	Dex file header
▷ struct string_id_list dex_string_ids	5502 strings	70h	55F8h	Fg:	Bg:	String ID list
▷ struct type_id_list dex_type_ids	789 types	5668h	C54h	Fg:	Bg:	Type ID list
▷ struct proto_id_list dex_proto_ids	1133 prototypes	62BCh	351Ch	Fg:	Bg:	Method prototype ID list
▷ struct field_id_list dex_field_ids	1556 fields	97D8h	30A0h	Fg:	Bg:	Field ID list
▷ struct method_id_list dex_method_ids	4358 methods	C878h	8830h	Fg:	Bg:	Method ID list
▷ struct class_def_item_list dex_class_defs	427 classes	150A8h	3560h	Fg:	Bg:	Class definitions list
▷ struct map_list_type dex_map_list	17 items	1995Ch	D0h	Fg:	Bg:	Map list

Figure 2-2   Highlighted header section of the classes.dex file

What we're primarily interested in is where the code lives. From the dex format specification we know that we need to navigate to the instructions section, which is deep within the classes section of the classes.dex file.

Using the 010 Editor, follow these steps to navigate to that section:

1. Go to struct class_def_item_list dex_class_defs for the list of class definitions.

2. Choose something simple, like the OnCreate method or in this case the com.riis.callqueuemanager.LoginActivity$1 method, so that we have a chance of reading and understanding the opcodes.

3. Find the struct class_data_item class_data structure, which contains all the information that the DVM needs to execute the constructor for the LoginActivity method.

4. Open the struct code_item code structure.

5. The six instructions that make up our <init> or constructor method are shown in Figure 2-3.

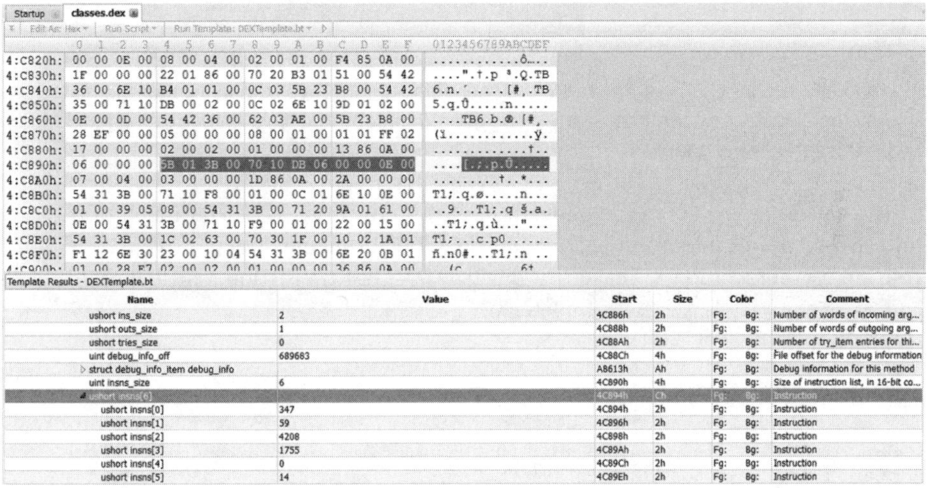

Figure 2-3   LoginActivity constructor

The opcode definition for each of these bytecodes is defined in https://source. android.com/devices/tech/dalvik/dalvik-bytecode.html. For example, the 5B that occurs at the start of the highlighted area is "input-object," while 5B 01 is "put the following object in register 1 of the DVM."

Reading the bytecodes at this level is not for the faint-hearted. Dexdump, which comes as part of the Android SDK, translates the method's bytes into assembler-like opcodes. Run the following command on the classes.dex file to get an assembler version of the opcodes.

```
dexdump.exe -d classes.dex
```

In Figure 2-4 we show the dexdump output for this method, and it should be clear that much of the original code information is beginning to reappear.

The key to unlocking this so that it's really close to the original code is dex2jar. The dex2jar tool takes these bytecodes, as well as the rest of the rich information in the classes.dex, and does a wonderful job of converting it into a Java classfile. It doesn't actually decompile the code, but once it's in a Java jar format it can be decompiled using any one of the many decompilers that are available, such as JD-GUI. Figure 2-5 shows the decompiled LoginActivity method.

Note

Although dex2jar changes the Android bytecode back into Java bytecode, there is no reason why the classes.dex can't be reverse engineered directly into Java source using jadx. More on this later in the chapter.

If we want to protect our code we'll need to know how to hide as much of this information as possible from dex2jar and JD-GUI. In the next section we'll show how you can use obfuscation to make this dex2jar/JD-GUI translation a little more difficult or, at the very least, less complete.

```
Class #253          -
  Class descriptor  : 'Lcom/riis/callqueuemanager/LoginActivity$1;'
  Access flags      : 0x0000 ()
  Superclass        : 'Ljava/lang/Object;'
  Interfaces        -
    #0              : 'Lcom/riis/callqueuemanager/broadsoftrequest/BroadsoftResponseListener;'
  Static fields     -
  Instance fields   -
    #0              : (in Lcom/riis/callqueuemanager/LoginActivity$1;)
      name          : 'this$0'
      type          : 'Lcom/riis/callqueuemanager/LoginActivity;'
      access        : 0x1010 (FINAL SYNTHETIC)
  Direct methods    -
    #0              : (in Lcom/riis/callqueuemanager/LoginActivity$1;)
      name          : '<init>'
      type          : '(Lcom/riis/callqueuemanager/LoginActivity;)V'
      access        : 0x10000 (CONSTRUCTOR)
      code          -
      registers     : 2
      ins           : 2
      outs          : 1
      insns size    : 6 16-bit code units
04c884:                |[04c884] com.riis.callqueuemanager.LoginActivity.1.<init>:(Lcom/riis/callqueuemanager/LoginActivity;)V
04c894: 5b01 3b00      |0000: iput-object v1, v0, Lcom/riis/callqueuemanager/LoginActivity$1;.this$0:Lcom/riis/callqueuemanager/LoginActivity;
04c898: 7010 db06 0000 |0002: invoke-direct {v0}, Ljava/lang/Object;.<init>:()V // method@06db
04c89e: 0e00           |0005: return-void
      catches         : (none)
      positions       :
        0x0000 line=1
        0x0002 line=106
      locals          :
        0x0000 - 0x0006 reg=0 this Lcom/riis/callqueuemanager/LoginActivity$1;
```

Figure 2-4   Dexdump output of `<init>`, showing bytecode highlighted and corresponding opcodes

Figure 2-5   Decompiled LoginActivity class

Obfuscation Best Practices

Obfuscators protect against decompilation in a number of ways. They don't stop decompilers or dex2jar from reverse engineering the code, but they do make the decompiled code harder to understand. At the very simplest, they convert all the variables and method names and strings in an APK into one or two character strings. This takes a lot of the meaning out of the Java source and makes it more difficult, for example, to find an API key or where you're storing the user's login information. Good obfuscators will also change the flow of the code and, in many cases, hide a lot of the business logic. It won't stop a determined hacker from understanding what you're doing in your code, but it will make it significantly harder.

Just like there are plenty of Java decompilers, there are also plenty of Java obfuscators, such as ProGuard, yGuard, RetroGuard, DashO, Allatori, Jshrink, Smokescreen, JODE, JavaGuard, Zelix Klassmaster, and jCloak, just to name a few. There is even an Android classes.dex obfuscator, called Apkfuscator, which is available at https://github.com/strazzere/APKfuscator, or you can try Shield4J at http://shield4j.com.

In this section we'll look at ProGuard, which ships with the Android SDK, as well as DexGuard, its commercial version.

Let's take a look at one of the samples from Google, in this case the SIP client for making phone calls called WalkieTalkie. You can download the Google samples using the Android SDK Manager; and to get Walkie Talkie code, download the samples for API 17. The sample we're looking for is called SipDemo.

Rather than look at the entire codebase, we can use the method initializeLocalProfile to see whether our obfuscation is effective or not. A good target is initializeLocalProfile because it shows the app saving our credentials, including the password, in the shared preferences, which we probably don't want anyone to see. Listing 2-1 shows the original Google code.

Listing 2-1 **Original initializeLocalProfile() code**

```
/**
     * Logs you into your SIP provider, registering this device as the location
     to
     * send SIP calls to for your SIP address.
     */
    public void initializeLocalProfile() {
        if (manager == null) {
            return;
        }

        if (me != null) {
            closeLocalProfile();
        }

        SharedPreferences prefs =
                PreferenceManager.getDefaultSharedPreferences(getBaseContext());
        String username = prefs.getString("namePref", "");
        String domain = prefs.getString("domainPref", "");
```

```
        String password = prefs.getString("passPref", "");

        if (username.length() == 0 || domain.length() == 0 || password.length()
        == 0) {
            showDialog(UPDATE_SETTINGS_DIALOG);
            return;
        }

        try {
            SipProfile.Builder builder = new SipProfile.Builder(username,
            domain);
            builder.setPassword(password);
            me = builder.build();

            Intent i = new Intent();
            i.setAction("android.SipDemo.INCOMING_CALL");
            PendingIntent pi = PendingIntent.getBroadcast(this, 0, i,
 Intent.FILL_IN_DATA);
            manager.open(me, pi, null);


            // This listener must be added AFTER manager.open is called,
            // Otherwise the methods aren't guaranteed to fire.

            manager.setRegistrationListener(me.getUriString(),
new SipRegistrationListener() {
                    public void onRegistering(String localProfileUri) {
                        updateStatus("Registering with SIP Server...");
                    }

                    public void onRegistrationDone(String localProfileUri,
long expiryTime) {
                            updateStatus("Ready");
                    }

                    public void onRegistrationFailed(String localProfileUri,
int errorCode,
                            String errorMessage) {
                        updateStatus("Registration failed.  Please check
                        settings.");
                    }
                });
        } catch (ParseException pe) {
            updateStatus("Connection Error.");
        } catch (SipException se) {
            updateStatus("Connection error.");
        }
    }
```

These days, more and more apps that we audit are using ProGuard for obfuscation, but until relatively recently most Android developers didn't know what ProGuard was let alone how to enable it. Let's take a look at what you can see first with no obfuscation.

No Obfuscation

Take the following steps to generate the APK and then decompile the source:

1. Compile the WalkieTalkie project.

2. Export the unsigned APK if you're using an IDE.

3. Run the command dex2jar WalkieTalkieActivity.apk.

4. Run the command jd-gui WalkieTalkieActivity_dex2jar.jar.

Listing 2-2 shows the decompiled code. As you can see, it is very close to the original code in Listing 2-1 except it is missing the comments.

Listing 2-2   **Decompiled initializeLocalProfile() code**

```
public void initializeLocalProfile()
  {
    if (this.manager == null)
      return;
    if (this.me != null)
      closeLocalProfile();
    SharedPreferences localSharedPreferences =
  PreferenceManager.getDefaultSharedPreferences(getBaseContext());
    String str1 = localSharedPreferences.getString("namePref", "");
    String str2 = localSharedPreferences.getString("domainPref", "");
    String str3 = localSharedPreferences.getString("passPref", "");
    if ((str1.length() == 0) || (str2.length() == 0) || (str3.length() == 0))
    {
      showDialog(3);
      return;
    }
    try
    {
      SipProfile.Builder localBuilder = new SipProfile.Builder(str1, str2);
      localBuilder.setPassword(str3);
      this.me = localBuilder.build();
      Intent localIntent = new Intent();
      localIntent.setAction("android.SipDemo.INCOMING _ CALL");
      PendingIntent localPendingIntent = PendingIntent.getBroadcast(this, 0,
      localIntent, 2);
      this.manager.open(this.me, localPendingIntent, null);
      this.manager.setRegistrationListener(this.me.getUriString(), new
      SipRegistrationListener()
      {
        public void onRegistering(String paramAnonymousString)
        {
          WalkieTalkieActivity.this.updateStatus("Registering with SIP Server...");
        }

        public void onRegistrationDone(String paramAnonymousString, long
        paramAnonymousLong)
        {
          WalkieTalkieActivity.this.updateStatus("Ready");
        }
```

```
      public void onRegistrationFailed(String paramAnonymousString1, int
      paramAnonymousInt, String paramAnonymousString2)
      {
        WalkieTalkieActivity.this.updateStatus("Registration failed.  Please
        check settings.");
      }
    });
    return;
  }
  catch (ParseException localParseException)
  {
    updateStatus("Connection Error.");
    return;
  }
  catch (SipException localSipException)
  {
    updateStatus("Connection error.");
  }
}
```

ProGuard

The ProGuard obfuscator ships with the Android SDK and is very easy to enable. Simply uncomment the line in the project.properties file that begins with proguard.config, as shown in Listing 2-3.

In the example that follows in this section, ProGuard is using two configuration files. The first is proguard-android.txt in the tools/proguard directory, which is the shared generic Android configuration file. The second is proguard-project.txt, which is the project configuration file. The latter is often left blank for basic obfuscation.

This only works with the Ant or Eclipse integration. In Android Studio you will need to configure ProGuard in build.gradle as follows:

```
buildTypes {
      release {
          runProguard false
          proguardFiles getDefaultProguardFile('proguard-android.txt'),
          'proguard-rules.txt'
      }
  }
```

Instead of "proguard-project.txt" for the specific project, Android Studio names it "proguard-rules.txt" but it still needs to be created and left blank. Instead of uncommenting, you need to change runProguard from false to true.

Listing 2-3   **Enabling ProGuard in the project.properties file**

```
# This file is automatically generated by Android Tools.
# Do not modify this file -- YOUR CHANGES WILL BE ERASED!
#
# This file must be checked in Version Control Systems.
#
# To customize properties used by the Ant build system edit
# "ant.properties", and override values to adapt the script to your
# project structure.
#
# To enable ProGuard to shrink and obfuscate your code, uncomment this
(available properties: sdk.dir, user.home):
proguard.config=${sdk.dir}/tools/proguard/proguard-android.txt:proguard-project.txt

# Project target.
target=android-19
```

ProGuard can be run from the command line or it integrates into your IDE, but it only runs when generating production APKs. It does not run when generating debug APKs. It's a common mistake to forget to check that your APK has been obfuscated before uploading it to Google Play, so always double-check by decompiling your APK to be extra sure that the obfuscation worked.

Note

The tools/proguard directory also contains a proguard-android-optimize.txt file for shrinking the APK as well as obfuscating it.

Let's see how effective ProGuard is in protecting our code. To do this, we need to run through basically the same series of steps as shown above to compile and then decompile the APK, but we must also make sure the proguard.config line has been uncommented. Finally, we need to sign the APK since it's a production APK. Assuming you're using an IDE such as Eclipse, take the following steps to generate the APK and then decompile the source.

1. Compile the WalkieTalkie project.

2. Generate your own keystore using the IDE Wizard.

3. Export the signed APK.

4. Run the command dex2jar WalkieTalkieActivity.apk.

5. Run the command jd-gui WalkieTalkieActivity_dex2jar.jar.

Listing 2-4 shows the fruits of your labors.

Listing 2-4 **Decompiled `initializeLocalProfile()` code with ProGuard
obfuscation**

```
public void b()
  {
    if (this.b == null)
      return;
    if (this.c != null)
      c();
    SharedPreferences localSharedPreferences = PreferenceManager.getDefaultShared
    Preferences(getBaseContext());
    String str1 = localSharedPreferences.getString("namePref", "");
    String str2 = localSharedPreferences.getString("domainPref", "");
    String str3 = localSharedPreferences.getString("passPref", "");
    if ((str1.length() == 0) || (str2.length() == 0) || (str3.length() == 0))
    {
      showDialog(3);
      return;
    }
    try
    {
      SipProfile.Builder localBuilder = new SipProfile.Builder(str1, str2);
      localBuilder.setPassword(str3);
      this.c = localBuilder.build();
      Intent localIntent = new Intent();
      localIntent.setAction("android.SipDemo.INCOMING _ CALL");
      PendingIntent localPendingIntent = PendingIntent.getBroadcast(this, 0,
      localIntent, 2);
      this.b.open(this.c, localPendingIntent, null);
      this.b.setRegistrationListener(this.c.getUriString(), new b(this));
      return;
    }
    catch (ParseException localParseException)
    {
      a("Connection Error.");
      return;
    }
    catch (SipException localSipException)
    {
      a("Connection error.");
    }
  }
```

As you can see, the method name and the variables have been changed. The intention here is to remove any information that would help the attacker understand how your code works. However, it's still obvious where the preferences are being stored.

If you ever need to get back to the original method names, ProGuard creates a mapping.txt file, which enables you to see exactly what method names and variables it transformed. We can see in Listing 2-5 just what has changed—in our example we can see that void `initializeLocalProfile()` has indeed changed to b.

Listing 2-5   **Mapping.txt**

```
  com.example.android.sip.IncomingCallReceiver ->
  com.example.android.sip.IncomingCallReceiver:

 void onReceive(android.content.Context,android.content.Intent) -> onReceive
com.example.android.sip.IncomingCallReceiver$1 -> com.example.android.sip.a:
    com.example.android.sip.IncomingCallReceiver this$0 -> a
    void onRinging(android.net.sip.SipAudioCall,android.net.sip.SipProfile) ->
onRinging
com.example.android.sip.SipSettings -> com.example.android.sip.SipSettings:
    void onCreate(android.os.Bundle) -> onCreate
com.example.android.sip.WalkieTalkieActivity ->
com.example.android.sip.WalkieTalkieActivity:

java.lang.String sipAddress -> a
    android.net.sip.SipManager manager -> b
    android.net.sip.SipProfile me -> c
    android.net.sip.SipAudioCall call -> d
    com.example.android.sip.IncomingCallReceiver callReceiver -> e
    void onCreate(android.os.Bundle) -> onCreate
    void onStart() -> onStart
    void onDestroy() -> onDestroy
    void initializeManager() -> a
    void initializeLocalProfile() -> b
    void closeLocalProfile() -> c
    void initiateCall() -> d
    void updateStatus(java.lang.String) -> a
    void updateStatus(android.net.sip.SipAudioCall) -> a

    boolean onTouch(android.view.View,android.view.MotionEvent) -> onTouch
    boolean onCreateOptionsMenu(android.view.Menu) -> onCreateOptionsMenu
    boolean onOptionsItemSelected(android.view.MenuItem) -> onOptionsItemSelected
    android.app.Dialog onCreateDialog(int) -> onCreateDialog
    void updatePreferences() -> e

com.example.android.sip.WalkieTalkieActivity$1 -> com.example.android.sip.b:
    com.example.android.sip.WalkieTalkieActivity this$0 -> a
    void onRegistering(java.lang.String) -> onRegistering
    void onRegistrationDone(java.lang.String,long) -> onRegistrationDone
    void onRegistrationFailed(java.lang.String,int,java.lang.String) ->
onRegistrationFailed

com.example.android.sip.WalkieTalkieActivity$2 -> com.example.android.sip.c:
    com.example.android.sip.WalkieTalkieActivity this$0 -> a
    void onCallEstablished(android.net.sip.SipAudioCall) -> onCallEstablished
    void onCallEnded(android.net.sip.SipAudioCall) -> onCallEnded

com.example.android.sip.WalkieTalkieActivity$3 -> com.example.android.sip.d:
    com.example.android.sip.WalkieTalkieActivity this$0 -> a
    java.lang.String val$status -> b
    void run() -> run
```

```
com.example.android.sip.WalkieTalkieActivity$4 -> com.example.android.sip.e:
    com.example.android.sip.WalkieTalkieActivity this$0 -> a
    android.view.View. val$textBoxView -> b
    void onClick(android.content.DialogInterface,int) -> onClick

com.example.android.sip.WalkieTalkieActivity$5 -> com.example.android.sip.f:
    com.example.android.sip.WalkieTalkieActivity this$0 -> a
    void onClick(android.content.DialogInterface,int) -> onClick

com.example.android.sip.WalkieTalkieActivity$6 -> com.example.android.sip.g:
    com.example.android.sip.WalkieTalkieActivity this$0 -> a
    void onClick(android.content.DialogInterface,int) -> onClick

com.example.android.sip.WalkieTalkieActivity$7 -> com.example.android.sip.h:
    com.example.android.sip.WalkieTalkieActivity this$0 -> a
    void onClick(android.content.DialogInterface,int) -> onClick
```

ProGuard creates four files to help you keep track. They are dump.txt, mapping.txt, seeds.txt, and usage.txt.

- dump.txt shows the Java Classfile information before it gets transformed into a classes.dex file.
- mapping.txt shows names before and after obfuscation changes.
- seeds.txt lists the classes not obfuscated.
- usage.txt lists the code that was removed from the APK.

You can find the ProGuard SDK in the sdk/tools/proguard directory of the Android SDK. It provides some extra ProGuard tools, such as retrace, which allows you to debug an obfuscated app in the field. Use the following command to give you a stacktrace output as if you never enabled obfuscation.

```
java -jar retrace.jar mapping.txt appname.trace
```

If you want to configure your own obfuscation, use the proguardgui (see Figure 2-6) in the tools/proguard/bin directory, as the configuration language in the ProGuard configuration files is a bit arcane.

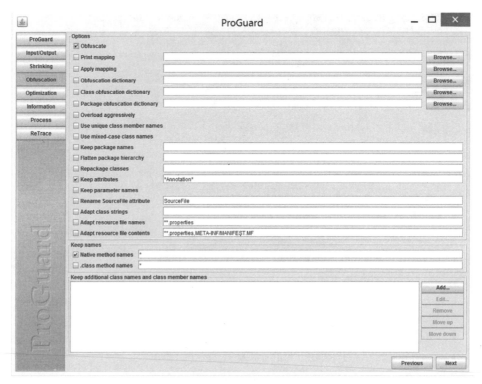

Figure 2-6 Decompiled ProGuard GUI

DexGuard

One of the best descriptions on the different levels of obfuscation comes from Christian Collberg's paper, "A Taxonomy of Obfuscating Transformations," which you can find at https://researchspace.auckland.ac.nz/bitstream/handle/2292/3491/TR148.pdf. A Java list of obfuscation classifications from the paper can be found in Table 2-1.

Table 2-1   **Taxonomy of Obfuscations**

Obfuscation Type	Classification	Transformation
Layout		Scramble identifiers.
Control	Computations	Insert dead or irrelevant code.
		Extend a loop condition.
		Reducible to nonreducible.
		Add redundant operands.
		Remove programming idioms.
		Parallelize code.
	Aggregations	Inline and outline methods.
		Interleave methods.
		Clone methods.
		Loop transformations.
	Ordering	Reorder statements.
		Reorder loops.
		Reorder expressions.
Data	Storage and encoding	Change encoding.
		Split variables.
		Convert static data to procedural data.
	Aggregation	Merge scalar variables.
		Factor a class.
		Insert a bogus class.
		Refactor a class.
		Split an array.
		Merge arrays.
		Fold an array.
		Flatten an array.
	Ordering	Reorder methods and instance variables.
		Reorder arrays.

Continues

Table 2-1   **Taxonomy of Obfuscations (*Continued*)**

Obfuscation Type	Classification	Transformation
Preventative	Targeted	HoseMocha
	Inherent	Add aliased formals to prevent slicing.
		Add variable dependencies to prevent slicing.
		Add bogus data dependencies.
		Use opaque predicates with side effects.
		Make opaque predicates using difficult theorems.

There are four major categories of obfuscation: layout, control, data, and preventative. We've already seen a good example where the identifiers have been scrambled, which is a good example of layout obfuscation. Control obfuscations try to modify the app's control flow to make it irreducible and hopefully break any link between the obfuscated and original code. Data obfuscations change the format of any data storage, and preventative obfuscations target the obfuscation tools to stop them from working in the first place.

Although ProGuard does some data and control transformations, it mostly scrambles identifiers, which does not protect your code anywhere near enough to let you sleep soundly, assured that your code is safe from prying eyes. The code structure and content in Listing 2-4 still looks too similar to the original code in Listing 2-1.

Thankfully, there are still some other options. One is commercial obfuscators, which do a lot more control—the data and preventative types. DashO from Preemptive Software and DexGuard are just two examples.

DexGuard comes from Eric Lafortune, who is the same person behind ProGuard. To enable DexGuard in Eclipse, take the following steps:

1. Download DexGuard from www.saikoa.com/dexguard.

2. Unzip and go to the Eclipse plug-in directory in dexguard/directory.

3. Copy the dexguard jar file com.saikoa.dexguard.eclipse.adt.jar into your adt/eclipse/plugins directory and restart Eclipse.

4. Right click on Android Tools->Export Optimized and Obfuscated Application Package (DexGuard) to export the APK.

If you now run dex2jar on the APK that's been protected by DexGuard you can see that the resulting jar file is only a fraction of the size of the other jar files and can't be decompiled using jd-gui. DexGuard has used a preventative obfuscation and targeted the dex2jar tool so that the APK cannot be decompiled. Round 1 to DexGuard.

However, as we mentioned before, dex2jar isn't really a decompiler—it's a bytecode translator from classes.dex to Java jar files, which are then subsequently decompiled. And there are some alternatives if we get stuck. Jadx is an Android decompiler, available from https://github.com/skylot/jadx. We can run it against our DexGuarded protected source to see if we can decompile it back into Java. Run the command as follows:

```
jadx WalkieTalkieActivityDexGuard.apk
```

The output is shown in Listing 2-6.

Although jadx made a good effort at other classes, it failed on the initializeLocal-Profile() method (see Listing 2-6), where it simply output the method bytecode similar to what we saw earlier using the 010 Editor. It's also much harder to see that the user's credentials are being stored in SharedPreferences. Round 2 to DexGuard.

Listing 2-6   **Decompiled `initializeLocalProfile()` code with DexGuard obfuscation**

```
private void ´() {
        throw new UnsupportedOperationException("Method not decompiled:
com.example.android.sip.WalkieTalkieActivity.´():void");
        /* JADX: method processing error */
/*
        Error: java.lang.NullPointerException
    at jadx.core.dex.nodes.BlockNode.isDominator(BlockNode.java:118)
    at jadx.core.utils.BlockUtils.isPathExists(BlockUtils.java:206)
    at jadx.core.utils.RegionUtils.hasPathThruBlock(RegionUtils.java:212)
    at jadx.core.dex.visitors.regions.ProcessTryCatchRegions.isHandlerPath(Process
TryCatchRegions.java:160)
    at jadx.core.dex.visitors.regions.ProcessTryCatchRegions.wrapBlocks(ProcessTry
CatchRegions.java:127)
    at jadx.core.dex.visitors.regions.ProcessTryCatchRegions.leaveRegion(ProcessTry
CatchRegions.java:104)
    at jadx.core.dex.visitors.regions.DepthRegionTraversal.traverseInternal(Depth
RegionTraversal.java:48)
    at jadx.core.dex.visitors.regions.DepthRegionTraversal.traverseInternal(Depth
RegionTraversal.java:46)
    at jadx.core.dex.visitors.regions.DepthRegionTraversal.traverseInternal(Depth
RegionTraversal.java:46)
    at jadx.core.dex.visitors.regions.DepthRegionTraversal.traverseInternal(Depth
RegionTraversal.java:46)
    at jadx.core.dex.visitors.regions.DepthRegionTraversal.traverseInternal(Depth
RegionTraversal.java:46)
    at jadx.core.dex.visitors.regions.DepthRegionTraversal.traverse(DepthRegion
Traversal.java:18)
    at jadx.core.dex.visitors.regions.RegionMakerVisitor.postProcessRegions(Region
MakerVisitor.java:46)
```

```
    at jadx.core.dex.visitors.regions.RegionMakerVisitor.visit(RegionMakerVisitor.
java:40)
    at jadx.core.dex.visitors.DepthTraversal.visit(DepthTraversal.java:27)
    at jadx.core.dex.visitors.DepthTraversal.visit(DepthTraversal.java:16)
    at jadx.core.ProcessClass.process(ProcessClass.java:22)
    at jadx.api.JadxDecompiler.processClass(JadxDecompiler.java:196)
    at jadx.api.JavaClass.decompile(JavaClass.java:59)
    at jadx.api.JadxDecompiler$1.run(JadxDecompiler.java:130)
    at java.util.concurrent.ThreadPoolExecutor.runWorker(ThreadPoolExecutor.
java:1142)
    at java.util.concurrent.ThreadPoolExecutor$Worker.run(ThreadPoolExecutor.
java:617)
    at java.lang.Thread.run(Thread.java:745)
*/
        /*
        private void `() {
            r6 _ this = this;
            r0 = r6.`;
            if (r0 != 0) goto L _ 0x0005;
        ·L _ 0x0004:
            return;
        L _ 0x0005:
            r0 = r6.`;
            if (r0 == 0) goto L _ 0x000c;
        L _ 0x0009:
            r6.`();
        L _ 0x000c:
            r0 = r6.getBaseContext();
            r0 = android.preference.PreferenceManager.getDefaultSharedPreferences
            (r0);
            r3 = r0;
            r1 = "namePref";
            r2 = "";
            r4 = r0.getString(r1, r2);
            r0 = "domainPref";
            r1 = "";
            r5 = r3.getString(r0, r1);
            r0 = "passPref";
            r1 = "";
            r3 = r3.getString(r0, r1);
            r0 = r4.length();
            if (r0 == 0) goto L _ 0x003f;
        L _ 0x0033:
            r0 = r5.length();
            if (r0 == 0) goto L _ 0x003f;
        L _ 0x0039:
            r0 = r3.length();
            if (r0 != 0) goto L _ 0x0044;
        L _ 0x003f:
            r0 = 3;
            r6.showDialog(r0);
            return;
        L _ 0x0044:
            r0 = new android.net.sip.SipProfile$Builder;      Catch:{ Parse
            Exception -> 0x007d, SipException -> 0x0089 }
```

```
      r0.<init>(r4, r5);    Catch:{ ParseException -> 0x007d, SipException ->
      0x0089 }
      r4 = r0;
      r0.setPassword(r3);      Catch:{ ParseException -> 0x007d, SipException
      -> 0x0089 }
      r0 = r4.build();    Catch:{ ParseException -> 0x007d, SipException ->
      0x0089 }
      r6.. = r0;  Catch:{ ParseException -> 0x007d, SipException -> 0x0089
      }
      r0 = new android.content.Intent;  Catch:{ ParseException -> 0x007d,
      SipException -> 0x0089 }
      r0.<init>();     Catch:{ ParseException -> 0x007d, SipException ->
      0x0089 }
      r3 = r0;
      r1 = "android.SipDemo.INCOMING _ CALL";
      r0.setAction(r1);     Catch:{ ParseException -> 0x007d, SipException ->
      0x0089 }
      r0 = 0;
      r1 = 2;
      r3 = android.app.PendingIntent.getBroadcast(r6, r0, r3, r1);  Catch:{
      ParseException -> 0x007d, SipException -> 0x0089 }
      r0 = r6.`;  Catch:{ ParseException -> 0x007d, SipException -> 0x0089 }
      r1 = r6..;  Catch:{ ParseException -> 0x007d, SipException -> 0x0089 }
      r2 = 0;
      r0.open(r1, r3, r2);     Catch:{ ParseException -> 0x007d, SipException
      -> 0x0089 }
      r0 = r6.`;  Catch:{ ParseException -> 0x007d, SipException -> 0x0089 }
      r1 = r6..;  Catch:{ ParseException -> 0x007d, SipException -> 0x0089 }
      r1 = r1.getUriString();    Catch:{ ParseException -> 0x007d,
      SipException -> 0x0089 }
      r2 = new o.`;     Catch:{ ParseException -> 0x007d, SipException ->
      0x0089 }
      r2.<init>(r6);     Catch:{ ParseException -> 0x007d, SipException ->
      0x0089 }
      r0.setRegistrationListener(r1, r2); Catch:{ ParseException -> 0x007d,
      SipException -> 0x0089 }
      return;
  L _ 0x007d:
      r4 = "Connection Error.";
      r3 = r6;
      r0 = new o..;
      r0.<init>(r3, r4);
      r6.runOnUiThread(r0);
      return;
  L _ 0x0089:
      r4 = "Connection error.";
      r3 = r6;
      r0 = new o..;
      r0.<init>(r3, r4);
      r6.runOnUiThread(r0);
      return;
    }
   */
}
```

Security Through Obscurity

An obfuscator's effectiveness is measured by how well they use the obfuscation transformations presented in Table 2-1 and how many of them they use. If an obfuscator only scrambles identifiers, then it's not going to be very effective. Better obfuscators reorder the bytecode to make it irreducible so that the contol flow cannot be reverse engineered—you can do this by taking adavantage of opcode language contructs that have no equivalent in Java. They typically also encrypt strings and manipulate the data structures to make them hard to understand. The obfuscator tool automates these and more transformations for you.

However, many of the transformations—what we could call defactoring, literally the opposite of refactoring—can be applied manually as part of your coding process. Really large methods are preferred, and the more unconnected the functionality the better. This is very hard for many developers to do, as most people try to write code so that the next developer working on the code can understand it. But a developer's skill in writing clean code is often counterproductive from a security perspective.

When we audit an app, the first thing we do is search for the string key, which is more often than not in a file called Crypt.java. Sometimes it's a simple key; sometimes it's an Android or Device ID.

The developer who wrote the following code probably thought there was no way anyone would be able to replicate his key. And, while there are obviously a lot of ingredients needed to create the key, finding the recipe was way too easy, negating all the effort.

```
String key = Build.BOARD + Build.BRAND + Build.CPU_ABI + Build.DEVICE +
    Build.DISPLAY + Build.FINGERPRINT + Build.HOST + Build.ID + Build.MANUFACTURER +
    Build.MODEL + Build.PRODUCT + Build.TAGS + Build.TYPE + Build.USER;
```

A much better approach would be to assemble the key by separating out these elements in many different unconnected methods. Obfuscate your code by making it more opaque and less easy for someone to understand.

Testing

If you are using obfuscation in your projects, then it's important to have a testing strategy that isn't destroyed by any obfuscation. Unit testing is difficult on an obfuscated APK, so run your unit tests before obfuscation if possible. However, obfuscation does some major surgery on your APK. By its very nature, obfuscation results in many methods and variables being renamed as well as significant changes made to the flow of your app, so you'll need to do some testing before releasing your app into Google Play with any confidence.

You can use the -applymapping and -printmapping options in ProGuard. These are typically used in incremental obfuscation when making patches to obfuscated code but can also be used for unit testing obfuscated code, not unlike using the retrace command earlier.

In the ProGuard configuration file of the main project, use the following directive:

```
-printmapping proguard-mapping.txt
```

And in the ProGuard configuration file of the test project, use the following directives:

```
-applymapping ../mainproject/bin/proguard-mapping.txt
-injars ../mainproject/bin/classes
```

ProGuard will now obfuscate the test files the same as the original code.

Another approach would be to use Behavior Driven Development (BDD) to complement your Test Driven Development (TDD); the standard framework for performing BDD testing is Cucumber. For Android you can use Calabash for your Cucumber tests, which is available at http://calaba.sh, and also see Chapter 6 for an example.

BDD tests at the activity level rather than at the method level, so obfuscation should not have any effect on your BDD tests. If the debug APK passes a series of BDD tests and your production APK does not, then you know your obfuscation needs to be dialed back a notch or two.

Smali

The Icelandic theme comes up again and again in Android. The Dalvik in DVM is the name of an Icelandic fishing village where the original developer of the DVM's ancestors came from. So, continuing with the Icelandic theme, there are also Baksmali and Smali, which are the de facto tools used to disassemble and assemble classes.dex files. Smali means shepherd or assembler in Icelandic, and Baksmali means disassembler. Disassembled files are given the .smali extension, where each Smali file corresponds to the original java file.

Note
ART replaces the DVM, and ART simply stands for Android Runtime.

Smali files are ASCII representation of the Dalvik opcodes and are fairly easy to read, similar in style and content to what we saw using dexdump earlier in the chapter. Smali is its own language, and there is no reason why you couldn't code your entire Android app in Smali if you had enough time. See http://source.android.com/devices /tech/dalvik/dalvik-bytecode.html for a good beginner's reference to Smali and the DVM.

Helloworld

Android provides its own HelloWorld app, which is the introduction to Android that most developers use. If you can't remember how to create it, then you can find directions at http://developer.android.com/training/basics/firstapp/index.html. Listing 2-7 shows the code.

Listing 2-7   **Android HelloWorld**

```
package com.example.myfirstapp;

import android.support.v7.app.ActionBarActivity;
import android.support.v4.app.Fragment;
import android.os.Bundle;
import android.view.LayoutInflater;
import android.view.Menu;
import android.view.MenuItem;
import android.view.View;
import android.view.ViewGroup;

public class MainActivity extends ActionBarActivity {

  @Override
  protected void onCreate(Bundle savedInstanceState) {
    super.onCreate(savedInstanceState);                        // line 18
    setContentView(R.layout.activity_main);                    // line 19

    if (savedInstanceState == null) {
      getSupportFragmentManager().beginTransaction()
          .add(R.id.container, new PlaceholderFragment()).commit();
    }
  }

  @Override
  public boolean onCreateOptionsMenu(Menu menu) {

    // Inflate the menu; this adds items to the action bar if it is present.
    getMenuInflater().inflate(R.menu.main, menu);
    return true;
  }

  @Override
  public boolean onOptionsItemSelected(MenuItem item) {
    // Handle action bar item clicks here. The action bar will
    // automatically handle clicks on the Home/Up button, so long
    // as you specify a parent activity in AndroidManifest.xml.
    int id = item.getItemId();
    if (id == R.id.action_settings) {
      return true;
    }
    return super.onOptionsItemSelected(item);
  }

  /**
   * A placeholder fragment containing a simple view.
   */
  public static class PlaceholderFragment extends Fragment {

    public PlaceholderFragment() {
    }

    @Override
    public View onCreateView(LayoutInflater inflater, ViewGroup container,
        Bundle savedInstanceState) {
```

```
        View rootView = inflater.inflate(R.layout.fragment_main, container,
            false);
        return rootView;
    }
  }

}
```

Once you have the HelloWorld app working in the emulator, download the APK using the following command:

```
adb pull /data/app/com.example.myfirstapp-1.apk
```

We can now disassemble the app into Smali using the apktool tool or using Baksmali directly (you can find links to these tools in Chapter 1). Run the following command to disassemble our APK:

```
java -jar baksmali.jar com.example.myfirstapp-1.apk
```

The disassembled Smali code is shown in Listing 2-8.

Listing 2-8   Smali HelloWorld code

```
.class public Lcom/example/myfirstapp/MainActivity;
.super Landroid/support/v7/app/ActionBarActivity;
.source "MainActivity.java"

# annotations
.annotation system Ldalvik/annotation/MemberClasses;
    value = {
        Lcom/example/myfirstapp/MainActivity$PlaceholderFragment;
    }
.end annotation

# direct methods
.method public constructor <init>()V
    .registers 1
    .line 0
    invoke-direct {p0}, Landroid/support/v7/app/ActionBarActivity;-><init>()V
    return-void
.end method
# virtual methods
.method protected onCreate(Landroid/os/Bundle;)V
    .registers 5
    .param p1, "savedInstanceState"    # Landroid/os/Bundle;

    .line 0
    invoke-super {p0, p1}, Landroid/support/v7/app/ActionBarActivity;->onCreate
    (Landroid/os/Bundle;)V

    .line 19
    const v0, 0x7f030018
    invoke-virtual {p0, v0}, Lcom/example/myfirstapp/MainActivity;->setContentView
    (I)V
```

```
    .line 21
    if-nez p1,
:cond_22    .line 22
invoke-virtual {p0}, Lcom/example/myfirstapp/MainActivity;-
>getSupportFragmentManager()Landroid/support/v4/app/FragmentManager;
move-result-object v0
    invoke-virtual {v0}, Landroid/support/v4/app/FragmentManager;->begin
    Transaction()Landroid/support/v4/app/FragmentTransaction;
    move-result-object v0
    .line 23
    new-instance v1, Lcom/example/myfirstapp/MainActivity$PlaceholderFragment;
    invoke-direct {v1}, Lcom/example/myfirstapp/MainActivity$PlaceholderFragment;-
    ><init>()V
    const v2, 0x7f05003c
    invoke-virtual {v0, v2, v1}, Landroid/support/v4/app/FragmentTransaction;-
    >add(ILandroid/support/v4/app/Fragment;)Landroid/support/v4/app/Fragment
    Transaction;
    move-result-object v0
    invoke-virtual {v0}, Landroid/support/v4/app/FragmentTransaction;->commit()I
    .line 25
    :cond_22
    return-void
.end method

.method public onCreateOptionsMenu(Landroid/view/Menu;)Z
    .registers 4
    .param p1, "menu"    # Landroid/view/Menu;

    .line 0
    invoke-virtual {p0}, Lcom/example/myfirstapp/MainActivity;->getMenuInflater()
    Landroid/view/MenuInflater;
    move-result-object v0
    const/high16 v1, 0x7f0c0000
    invoke-virtual {v0, v1, p1}, Landroid/view/MenuInflater;->inflate(ILandroid/
    view/Menu;)V
    .line 32
    const/4 v0, 0x1
    return v0
.end method
.method public onOptionsItemSelected(Landroid/view/MenuItem;)Z
    .registers 4
    .param p1, "item"    # Landroid/view/MenuItem;
    .line 0
 invoke-interface {p1}, Landroid/view/MenuItem;->getItemId()I
    move-result v1

    .line 41
    .local v1, "id":I
    const v0, 0x7f05003d
    if-ne v1, v0, :cond_b
    .line 42
    const/4 v0, 0x1
    return v0
    .line 44
    :cond_b
```

```
    invoke-super {p0, p1}, Landroid/support/v7/app/ActionBarActivity;-
>onOptionsItemSelected(Landroid/view/MenuItem;)Z
    move-result v0
    return v0
.end method
```

Compare lines 18 and 19 of the Java code of the HelloWorld app with the corresponding Smali.

```
super.onCreate(savedInstanceState);
setContentView(R.layout.activity _ main);
```

These statements correspond to lines 0 and 19 of the Smali code, where p1 is savedInstanceState and v0 or const 0x7f030018 is the activity_main, which we can find in the R.java file. The const 0x7f030018 is generated by the Android framework.

```
    .registers 5
    .param p1, "savedInstanceState"     # Landroid/os/Bundle;
    .line 0
    invoke-super {p0, p1}, Landroid/support/v7/app/ActionBarActivity;-
>onCreate(Landroid/os/Bundle;)V

    .line 19
    const v0, 0x7f030018
    invoke-virtual {p0, v0}, Lcom/example/myfirstapp/MainActivity;->setContentView(I)V
```

We can quickly determine that the disassembled code is again similar to the dex-dump output. It's difficult, but not impossible, to understand. And again, there is scope to cause havoc.

Remove App Store Check

Disassemblers were commonly used hacking tools in the 80s and 90s to crack an unlicensed copy of an application. A quick edit of an if statement or two, flip a Boolean from true to false on a license check, and the app is suddenly licensed.

We can disassemble the APK into Smali code using backsmali.jar, make modifications to the Smali code, reassemble it using smali.jar, and then resign it using jarsigner to create our own fake version of an APK.

Let's look at how we would remove some licensing code to use our fake APK somewhere that the original developers didn't want it used. Returning to our SIP app from earlier, let's first add some code to only let the Android app work if it's downloaded from Google Play.

To protect against your APK being uploaded onto an App Store other than Google Play, you can use a simple packagemanager check. We add this to our WalkieTalkie SIP example from earlier (refer to Listing 2-4). If the APK is installed from Google Play, the call to getInstallerPackageName() will return the string "com.google.android.feedback". So in our code we just exit the app if we don't see that string (see Listing 2-9). Installing the APK using adb or from any other app store other than Google Play means that that app will fail to run.

Listing 2-9   Check to see if APK was downloaded from Google Play

```
public static void validatePlayStoreInstaller(Context context) {
    PackageManager pm = context.getPackageManager();
    String installer = pm.getInstallerPackageName(context
        .getApplicationInfo().packageName);

    if(!"com.google.android.feedback".equals(installer)){
        System.exit(1);
    }
}
```

Note

You can simulate installing it from Google Play using the following command:

```
adb install -i com.google.android.feedback com.example.android.sip
```

Let's take a look at the disassembled package manager check in Smali (see Listing 2-10). The interesting code is between line 117 and line 118. If we change if-nez v0, :cond_0 to if-eqz v0, :cond_0 then we have removed our app store check. We need to reassemble our modified code and take the extra step of signing the APK, and we should now be able to run our app again by installing it using adb.

Listing 2-10   Disassembled `validatePlayStoreInstaller`

```
.method public static validatePlayStoreInstaller(Landroid/content/Context;)V
    .locals 3
    .parameter "context"

    .line 113
    invoke-virtual {p0}, Landroid/content/Context;->getPackageManager()Landroid/
    content/pm/PackageManager;

    move-result-object v1

    .line 114
    .line 115
    .local v1, pm:Landroid/content/pm/PackageManager;
    invoke-virtual {p0}, Landroid/content/Context;->getApplicationInfo()Landroid/
    content/pm/ApplicationInfo;

    move-result-object v0

    iget-object v0, v0, Landroid/content/pm/ApplicationInfo;->packageName:Ljava/
    lang/String;
```

```
    .line 114
    invoke-virtual {v1, v0}, Landroid/content/pm/PackageManager;->getInstaller
    PackageName(Ljava/lang/String;)Ljava/lang/String;

    move-result-object v2

    .line 117
    .local v2, installer:Ljava/lang/String;
    const-string v0, "com.google.android.feedback"

    invoke-virtual {v0, v2}, Ljava/lang/String;->equals(Ljava/lang/Object;)Z

    move-result v0

    if-nez v0, :cond_0

    .line 118
    const/4 v0, 0x1

    invoke-static {v0}, Ljava/lang/System;->exit(I)V

    .line 120
    :cond_0
    return-void
.end method.
```

The steps to reassemble, sign, and install the APK are as follows. We'll use apktool instead of smali.jar because it skips a couple steps:

1. java –jar apktool.jar b com.example.sip-1

2. keytool –genkey –v –keystore my-release-key.keystore –alias alias_name –keyalg RSA –validity 10000

3. jarsigner –verbose –keystore my-release-key.keystore ./com.example.sip-1/dist /com.example.sip-1.apk alias_name

4. adb install com.example.sip-1.apk

The app now runs, and it will always run unless it's downloaded from Google Play. We can also disassemble our earlier WalkieTalkie APK that was obfuscated with DexGuard (see Listing 2-11). DexGuard has obfuscated many of the variables, so although it's harder to read, there isn't anything to stop someone who is manipulating the code to see what insecurities might be exposed. The shared preference references are again a visible target, as you can see in line 124.

Listing 2-11 Disassembled `initializeLocalProfile()` protected with DexGuard

```
.method private ?()V
    .registers 7
    .line 0
    iget-object v0, p0, Lcom/example/android/sip/WalkieTalkieActivity;->?:Landroid/
    net/sip/SipManager;
    if-nez v0, :cond_5
    .line 116
    return-void
    .line 119
    :cond_5
    iget-object v0, p0, Lcom/example/android/sip/WalkieTalkieActivity;->?:Landroid/
    net/sip/SipProfile;
    if-eqz v0, :cond_c
    .line 120
    invoke-direct {p0}, Lcom/example/android/sip/WalkieTalkieActivity;->?()V
    .line 123
    :cond_c
    invoke-virtual {p0}, Lcom/example/android/sip/WalkieTalkieActivity;->getBase
    Context()Landroid/content/Context;
    move-result-object v0
    invoke-static {v0}, Landroid/preference/PreferenceManager;->getDefaultShared
    Preferences(Landroid/content/Context;)Landroid/content/SharedPreferences;
    move-result-object v0
    .line 124
    move-object v3, v0
    const-string v1, "namePref"
    const-string v2, ""
    invoke-interface {v0, v1, v2}, Landroid/content/SharedPreferences;->getString
    (Ljava/lang/String;Ljava/lang/String;)Ljava/lang/String;
    move-result-object v4
    .line 125
    const-string v0, "domainPref"
    const-string v1, ""
    invoke-interface {v3, v0, v1}, Landroid/content/SharedPreferences;->getString(
    Ljava/lang/String;Ljava/lang/String;)Ljava/lang/String;
    move-result-object v5
    .line 126
    const-string v0, "passPref"
    const-string v1, ""
    invoke-interface {v3, v0, v1}, Landroid/content/SharedPreferences;->getString(
    Ljava/lang/String;Ljava/lang/String;)Ljava/lang/String;
    move-result-object v3
    .line 128
    invoke-virtual {v4}, Ljava/lang/String;->length()I
    move-result v0
    if-eqz v0, :cond_3f
    invoke-virtual {v5}, Ljava/lang/String;->length()I
    move-result v0
    if-eqz v0, :cond_3f
    invoke-virtual {v3}, Ljava/lang/String;->length()I
    move-result v0
    if-nez v0, :cond_44
    .line 129
    :cond_3f
    const/4 v0, 0x3
```

```
invoke-virtual {p0, v0}, Lcom/example/android/sip/WalkieTalkieActivity;->show
Dialog(I)V
.line 130
return-void
.line 134
:cond_44
:try_start_44
new-instance v0, Landroid/net/sip/SipProfile$Builder;
invoke-direct {v0, v4, v5}, Landroid/net/sip/SipProfile$Builder;-><init>(Ljava
/lang/String;Ljava/lang/String;)V
.line 135
move-object v4, v0
invoke-virtual {v0, v3}, Landroid/net/sip/SipProfile$Builder;->setPassword
(Ljava/lang/String;)Landroid/net/sip/SipProfile$Builder;
.line 136
invoke-virtual {v4}, Landroid/net/sip/SipProfile$Builder;->build()Landroid/net/
sip/SipProfile;
move-result-object v0
iput-object v0, p0, Lcom/example/android/sip/WalkieTalkieActivity;->?:Landroid/
net/sip/SipProfile;
.line 138
new-instance v0, Landroid/content/Intent;
invoke-direct {v0}, Landroid/content/Intent;-><init>()V
.line 139
move-object v3, v0
const-string v1, "android.SipDemo.INCOMING_CALL"
invoke-virtual {v0, v1}, Landroid/content/Intent;->setAction(Ljava/lang/String;)
Landroid/content/Intent;
.line 140
const/4 v0, 0x0
const/4 v1, 0x2
invoke-static {p0, v0, v3, v1}, Landroid/app/PendingIntent;->getBroadcast
(Landroid/content/Context;ILandroid/content/Intent;I)Landroid/app/Pending
Intent;
move-result-object v3
.line 141
iget-object v0, p0, Lcom/example/android/sip/WalkieTalkieActivity;->?:Landroid/
net/sip/SipManager;
iget-object v1, p0, Lcom/example/android/sip/WalkieTalkieActivity;->?:Landroid/
net/sip/SipProfile;
const/4 v2, 0x0
invoke-virtual {v0, v1, v3, v2}, Landroid/net/sip/SipManager;->open(Landroid/
net/sip/SipProfile;Landroid/app/PendingIntent;Landroid/net/sip/SipRegistration
Listener;)V
.line 147
iget-object v0, p0, Lcom/example/android/sip/WalkieTalkieActivity;->?:Landroid/
net/sip/SipManager;
iget-object v1, p0, Lcom/example/android/sip/WalkieTalkieActivity;->?:Landroid/
net/sip/SipProfile;
invoke-virtual {v1}, Landroid/net/sip/SipProfile;->getUriString()Ljava/lang/
String;
move-result-object v1
new-instance v2, Lo/?;
invoke-direct {v2, p0}, Lo/?;-><init>(Lcom/example/android/sip/WalkieTalkie
Activity;)V
invoke-virtual {v0, v1, v2}, Landroid/net/sip/SipManager;->setRegistration
Listener(Ljava/lang/String;Landroid/net/sip/SipRegistrationListener;)V
```

```
:try_end_7c
.catch Ljava/text/ParseException; {:try_start_44 .. :try_end_7c} :catch
_7d
.catch Landroid/net/sip/SipException; {:try_start_44 .. :try_end_7c}
:catch_89
.line 161
return-void
.line 162
:catch_7d
const-string v4, "Connection Error."
move-object v3, p0
new-instance v0, Lo/?;
invoke-direct {v0, v3, v4}, Lo/?;-><init>(Lcom/example/android/sip/WalkieTalkie
Activity;Ljava/lang/String;)V
invoke-virtual {p0, v0}, Lcom/example/android/sip/WalkieTalkieActivity;->runOn
UiThread(Ljava/lang/Runnable;)V
return-void
.line 163
.line 164
:catch_89
const-string v4, "Connection error."
move-object v3, p0
new-instance v0, Lo/?;
invoke-direct {v0, v3, v4}, Lo/?;-><init>(Lcom/example/android/sip/Walkie
TalkieActivity;Ljava/lang/String;)V
invoke-virtual {p0, v0}, Lcom/example/android/sip/WalkieTalkieActivity;->runOn
UiThread(Ljava/lang/Runnable;)V
.line 166
return-void
.end method.
```

So there really isn't much we can do here to protect our APK. Obfuscation will only protect you from decompiling the APK, not from disassembling it. The good news is that it's a lot harder to understand Smali, so it's going to be orders of magnitude harder to hack than decompiled Java code. It will limit, but not eliminate, any security issues that might be exposed.

Hiding Business Rules in the NDK

Many Android apps contain business logic that may have taken many years to develop, and not understanding the repercussions of others being able to decompile your Android app means essentially giving away all that work for free.

Some examples that I've come across recently are connecting to a Bluetooth device in a car that had a proprietary data stream and connecting to a VoIP server API to make phone calls. The value of both of these apps is based on the business logic to allow the user to easily connect to external systems. The apps are not as attractive anymore if there are other cheaper apps on the marketplace that have copied this code.

The Native Developer Kit (NDK) enables developers to write code as a C++ library. This can be useful if you want to try to hide any business rules code in binary.

Unlike Java code, C++ cannot be decompiled, only disassembled. It's not enough to stop someone from reading the binary, but it does put the Android app's code on a par with Objective-C in iOS devices. Yes, you can still open the file using a hexadecimal editor or a tool like IDA Pro, but no one will be able to decompile back into code as easy to read as the original C++.

We'll cover the NDK in more detail in Chapter 5.

Conclusion

We've seen how easy it is to remove an APK from a phone. We've made several attempts at making it more and more difficult to decompile the code by using increasingly stronger versions of obfuscation. We've seen how someone can manipulate your APK by disassembling it and editing the Smali and then reassembling it to change its behavior. However, none of these completely protect the code. They raise the bar, quite high in some cases, but they all come with risks such that determined hackers with some time on their hands can debug your app and get at your code.

But what if you put it elsewhere? It's perfectly acceptable—with one caveat—to keep your most important code on a backend server. We will look at this in more detail in Chapter 6.

Authentication

In this chapter we look at how some of the authentication mechanisms have failed and what developers have been using to log in to mobile apps that has been more effective.

Secure Logins

Providing a secure login mechanism for your users is harder than on the Web. The trend on mobile devices is to make things as easy as possible for the user. Mobile keyboards are also small, so it's unlikely that someone is going to enter more than six characters to log in to an app.

But if you make it too easy to log in to your app, you run the risk of unauthorized users gaining access to sensitive data by going around this authentication.

The following tokens are common on Android devices as part of the login process:

- Username and password
- Device information, such as DeviceID and AndroidID
- Network information, such as IP address

The classic login of username and password is still the most common authentication on an Android phone.

Many apps ask to remember your username for the next login. This approach isn't recommended because it means the username is typically stored somewhere on the device.

Much worse, however, is when the app asks to remember the password when you log in because there is effectively no login the second time around (see Figure 3-1).

The app is caching the username and password, and it's probably being stored in the shared preferences or a client-side database. The app may also be using device-specific information, such as the AndroidID or an IP address, to log in each subsequent time.

Figure 3-1   Goatdroid login screen

In Listing 3-1 we see that the goatdroid username and password have been stored in cleartext in the shared preferences. We saw in Chapter 1 how easy it is for someone to back up a user's data and have access to the shared preferences folder.

Listing 3-1   **Credentials.xml**

```
<?xml version='1.0' encoding='utf-8' standalone='yes' ?>
<map>
<string name="password">goatdroid</string>
<boolean name="remember" value="true" />
<string name="username">goatdroid</string>
</map>
```

The code in Listing 3-2 shows that the user is permanently logged in to the app using only the DeviceID for authentication.

Listing 3-2   **DeviceID authentication**

```
public Login isAuthValidOrDeviceAuthorized (String authToken, String deviceID) {

    Login login = new Login();
    ArrayList<String> errors = new ArrayList<String>();
    if (!Validators.validateDeviceID(deviceID))
        errors.add(Constants.INVALID_DEVICE_ID);
    try {
        if (errors.size() == 0){
            if (isAuthValid(authToken)) {
                login.setSuccess(true);
            } else {
                if (dao.isDevicePermanentlyAuthorized(deviceID)) {
                    String newAuthToken = Utils.generateAutToken();
                    doa.updateAuthrizedDeviceAuth(deviceID, newAuthToken);
                    login.setAuthToken(newAuthToken);
                    login.setUserName(dao.getUserName(newAuthToken));
                    login.setAccountNumber(dao.getAccountNumber(newAuthToken));
                    login.setSuccess(true);
                }
            }
        }
    } catch (Exception e) {
        errors.add(Constants.UNEXPECTED_ERROR);
    } finally {
        login.setErrors(errors);
    }
    return login;
}
```

Even if you require a username and password, be aware that users often use the same username and password for multiple websites and mobile apps, so a certain level of vigilance needs to be enforced. Hardly a week goes by without some announcement of yet another website hack where millions of usernames and passwords have been stolen.

The Adobe website hack where 38 million usernames were stolen from Adobe (http://blogs.wsj.com/digits/2013/11/11/after-adobe-hack-other-sites-re-set-passwords/), the 5 million gmail usernames and passwords posted online (http://time.com/3318853/google-user-logins-bitcoin/), and many other similar stories mean that any usernames and passwords hacked on other sites may also be compromised on your site.

It's typically only a matter of time before these hacked usernames and passwords start to appear on torrent sites similar to what happened a few years ago with the Gawker website hack.

If you find lots of your usernames in these torrent files, then you need to prompt your users with the same username to reset their password. You can do this preferably via a well-crafted email or, better still, create a temporary password and get them to retrieve it via email before they can log in again. The WordPress follow-up after the gmail hack is a good example to follow on how to manage this type of messaging: http://en.blog.wordpress.com/2014/09/12/gmail-password-leak-update/. We'll talk more about this later.

Understanding Best Practices for User Authentication and Account Validation

Lets look at some best practices for user authentication. These practices come from what we've seen work and not work during our audits. The best practices are as follows:

- No password caching
- Minimum password length
- Validate email addresses
- Multi-factor authentication
- Server-side as well as client-side authentication

Do not save or cache username, and especially password, information on the phone, as there is always a risk that it will be found and decrypted. Even if you're encrypting the password, if you're also storing the key in the APK then it's going to be unencrypted. It is better not to store passwords, if you can get away with it, and make the user log in each time. We've also come across several apps that encrypt the password in shared preferences and then leave it in cleartext somewhere else, such as the database. This shows that mobile applications are growing organically with more than one team of developers, possibly in different countries. Without a good code review process a single developer can wreak havoc with security.

Try to enforce a minimum password length—passwords of less than six characters are highly prone to a brute force attack. Financial apps should have stricter policies than gaming apps.

Validate email addresses—you may need it later. This can be done either using regular expressions or via an email link during setup or, better still, using both approaches.

If you do update your password standards, notify your existing customers when they log in again to update their passwords.

It's becoming very common for websites to use two-factor authentication where a randomly generated PIN number is sent via SMS message to your phone before you can log in to the website. While this isn't going to work on mobile apps, we do know that it's easy to find the device ID, IP address, and location information to add extra layers of information.

Access control doesn't end at the client; it needs to be enforced at the server, too. Some back-end servers mistakenly rely on the client app to perform all authentication and assume that the web server does not need to do any authentication. Authenticate all API calls to paid resources. The server should also check for valid credentials each time or use a session token once again over SSL. It should also check for unusual activity, such as someone performing a brute force attack, and notify the user via email of unusual login activity.

If you are saving any personal, healthcare, or financial information, you should use an asymmetric or public/private key. This does require a round trip back to the server to decrypt the data, but if the phone is compromised the user's data will remain secure. Only the private key can decrypt the data, and that should never be stored on the phone.

Now let's look at how you might want to create better authentication for your app. Each example gets successively more complicated.

Take 1

In the first example, we have a basic login screen asking for username, password, and email address (see Listing 3-3). We're going to show how to check that they're not empty and then throw up an alert dialog. If you don't enter any data, then the alert dialog pops up (see line 44).

Listing 3-3   **Validate text fields**

```
package com.riis.login;

import android.os.Bundle;
import android.app.Activity;
import android.view.View;
import android.widget.Button;
import android.widget.EditText;

public class LoginActivity extends Activity {

    private Button loginButton;

    @Override
    protected void onCreate(Bundle savedInstanceState) {
        super.onCreate(savedInstanceState);
        setContentView(R.layout.login _ screen);

        initializeViews();
        bindListenersToVies();

    }

    private void initializeViews() {
        loginButton = (Button) findViewById(R.id.login _ button);

    }

    private void bindListenersToViews() {
```

```
          loginButton.setOnClickListener(new View.OnClickListener() {
              @Override
              public void onClick(View v) {
                      loginToApp();
              }
      });
      }

      private void loginToApp() {
          EditText usernameField = (EditText) findViewById(R.id.username_field);
          EditText passwordField = (EditText) findViewById(R.id.password_field);
          EditText emailField = (EditText) findViewById(R.id.email_field);


          if(areFieldsEmpty(usernameField, passwordField, emailField)) {
              AlertDialogs.showEmptyFieldsAlertDialog(this);
              // line 44
              return;
          }
      }

      private boolean areFieldsEmpty(EditText... fields) {
          for(int i = 0; i < fields.length; i++) {
              if(fields[i].getText().toString().matches("")) {
                  return true;
              }
          }

          return false;
      }

}
```

Take 2

If you're going to create your own login policy you might want to make sure that passwords are a certain length, so in the second example (see Listing 3-4) we're going to add a minimum password length of six. The code to check the length is straightforward (see line 95). I've also added a method, invalidEmail, to make sure that the email address is valid using the following regular expression (see line 78).

```
String EMAIL_PATTERN = "^[_A-Za-z0-9-]+(\\.[_A-Za-z0-9-]+)*@[A-Za-z0-9]+(\\.[A-Za-z0-9]+)*(\\.[A-Za-z]{2,})$";
```

From personal experience I should point out that if you're writing a method to check emails, or indeed any other authentication, then you should always make the default return what you would expect it to be for a failing or negative condition. In this case it's returning a true for an invalid email by default.

Listing 3-4   **Email validation**

```
package com.riis.validatelogin;

import java.util.regex.Matcher;
import java.util.regex.Pattern;

import com.riis.validatelogin.AlertDialogs;

import android.os.Bundle;
import android.app.Activity;
import android.util.Log;
import android.view.View;
import android.widget.Button;
import android.widget.EditText;

public class LoginActivity extends Activity {

    private Button loginButton;
    public static final String APP_TAG = "com.riis.validatelogin";
    public static final int MinPassLen = 6;

    @Override
    protected void onCreate(Bundle savedInstanceState) {
        super.onCreate(savedInstanceState);
        setContentView(R.layout.login_screen);

        initializeViews();
        bindListenersToVies();

    }

    private void initializeViews() {
        loginButton = (Button) findViewById(R.id.login_button);

    }

    private void bindListenersToVies() {
        loginButton.setOnClickListener(new View.OnClickListener() {
            @Override
            public void onClick(View v) {
                    loginToApp();
            }
    });
    }

    private void loginToApp() {
        EditText usernameField = (EditText) findViewById(R.id.username_field);
        EditText passwordField = (EditText) findViewById(R.id.password_field);
        EditText emailField = (EditText) findViewById(R.id.email_field);

        if(areFieldsEmpty(usernameField, passwordField, emailField)) {
                AlertDialogs.showEmptyFieldsAlertDialog(this);
```

```
                    return;
                }

            if(invalidEmail(emailField)) {
                AlertDialogs.showBadEmailAlertDialog(this);
                return;
            }

            if(shortPassword(passwordField)) {
                AlertDialogs.showBadPasswordAlertDialog(this,MinPassLen);
                return;
            }
        }



        private boolean areFieldsEmpty(EditText... fields) {
            for(int i = 0; i < fields.length; i++) {
                    if(fields[i].getText().toString().matches("")) {
                        Log.d(APP_TAG,"Empty Field");
                         return true;
                    }
            }
            return false;
        }


        private boolean invalidEmail(EditText email) {
            Pattern pattern;
            Matcher matcher;                                       //line 78
            String EMAIL_PATTERN = "^[_A-Za-z0-9-]+(\\.[_A-Za-z0-9-]+)*@[A-Za-z0-9]+(\\.
            [A-Za-z0-9]+)*(\\.[A-Za-z]{2,})$";
            pattern = Pattern.compile(EMAIL_PATTERN);
            matcher = pattern.matcher(email.getText().toString());
            if(matcher.matches()){
                Log.d(APP_TAG,"Valid Email" + matcher);
                return false;
            }
            Log.d(APP_TAG,"Invalid Email" + matcher);
            return true;
        }

        private boolean shortPassword(EditText passwordField) {

            if(passwordField.getText().toString().length() > (MinPassLen-1)){ // line 95
                Log.d(APP_TAG,"Valid Password");
                return false;
            }
            Log.d(APP_TAG,"Invalid Password");
            return true;
        }


    }
```

Take 3

In the next example (see Listing 3-5), I've added a check to see if the app on the phone or device has been used before, courtesy of its AndroidID. What I'm not suggesting here is that you use the AndroidID as a replacement for the user's login and password; rather, think about using it to supplement the authentication process.

If an app caches the username and password so you don't have to enter the password when you open the app, then it's stored somewhere on the phone and your app is probably insecure.

The AndroidID is not a secure token; in our example you should be able to see that it is easy to spoof creating a fake shared preferences file to make the app think it's on a different device.

I use the Android ID in our example; this is 64-bit number or UUID that is randomly generated on the device's first boot and should remain constant for the lifetime of the device.

I'm not using the DeviceID for a number of reasons. Wi-fi-only devices' telephony hardware just doesn't have a DeviceID. Also, the DeviceID will still be the same after device data wipes and factory resets. In my opinion, an app should regard this as a new device, but if you're using the DeviceID you won't be able to tell. Also, asking for a DeviceID requires a READ_PHONE_STATE permission, which may irritate your users if you don't otherwise use or need telephony.

The only downside of using the AndroidID instead of a DeviceID is that it's no good for Android 2.2 and below.

In the example, I'm writing out the AndroidID to a shared preferences file. When the user logs in for a second time it checks to see whether the AndroidID is in the shared preferences folder. This should be treated as an extra layer of authentication; for example, if you can't find the AndroidID then you know that it's a new user, so you should direct the user to the registration pages. Or, if it's not a new user, you should ask some of those "maiden name of your mother" security questions that you captured during the registration process.

Feel free to add more layers, such as checking the IP address as well as the AndroidID, using combinations of phone-specific Build attributes such as Build.Model. Or, you can use the IP address to check location using any of the GeoIP databases that are available and deny access if the location is in a different continent from the last login.

Listing 3-5   **Adding AndroidID validation**

```
package com.riis.validatephone;
import java.util.regex.Matcher;
import java.util.regex.Pattern;

import com.riis.validatephone.AlertDialogs;
```

```
import android.os.Bundle;
import android.provider.Settings.Secure;
import android.app.Activity;
import android.content.SharedPreferences;
import android.util.Log;
import android.view.View;
import android.widget.Button;
import android.widget.EditText;
import android.content.Context;

public class LoginActivity extends Activity {

    private Button loginButton;
    private SharedPreferences sharedPrefs;

    public static final String APP_TAG = "com.riis.validatephone";
    public static final int MinPassLen = 6;
    public static final String SHARED_PREF_NAME = "mySharedPrefs";
    public static final String DEVICE_ID = "lastDevice";
    public static String androidID = "";
    public static String spAndroidID = "";


    @Override
    protected void onCreate(Bundle savedInstanceState) {
        super.onCreate(savedInstanceState);
        setContentView(R.layout.login_screen);

        sharedPrefs = getSharedPreferences(SHARED_PREF_NAME, MODE_PRIVATE);

        initializeViews();
        bindListenersToViews();

    }

    private void initializeViews() {
        loginButton = (Button) findViewById(R.id.login_button);

    }

    private void bindListenersToViews() {
        loginButton.setOnClickListener(new View.OnClickListener() {
            @Override
            public void onClick(View v) {
                    loginToApp();
            }
    });
    }

    private void loginToApp() {
        EditText usernameField = (EditText) findViewById(R.id.username_field);
        EditText passwordField = (EditText) findViewById(R.id.password_field);
        EditText emailField = (EditText) findViewById(R.id.email_field);

        if(areFieldsEmpty(usernameField, passwordField, emailField)) {
                AlertDialogs.showEmptyFieldsAlertDialog(this);
```

```
            return;
    }

    if(invalidEmail(emailField)) {
        AlertDialogs.showBadEmailAlertDialog(this);
        return;
    }

    if(shortPassword(passwordField)) {
        AlertDialogs.showBadPasswordAlertDialog(this,MinPassLen);
        return;
    }

    getDeviceID();

}

private boolean areFieldsEmpty(EditText... fields) {
    for(int i = 0; i < fields.length; i++) {
            if(fields[i].getText().toString().matches("")) {
                    Log.d(APP_TAG,"Empty Field");
                     return true;
            }
    }
    return false;
}

private boolean invalidEmail(EditText email) {
    Pattern pattern;
    Matcher matcher;
    String EMAIL_PATTERN = "^[_A-Za-z0-9-]+(\\.[_A-Za-z0-9-]+)*@[A-Za-z0-9]+(\\.
    [A-Za-z0-9]+)*(\\.[A-Za-z]{2,})$";
    pattern = Pattern.compile(EMAIL_PATTERN);
    matcher = pattern.matcher(email.getText().toString());
    if(matcher.matches()){
        Log.d(APP_TAG,"Valid Email" + matcher);
        return false;
    }
    Log.d(APP_TAG,"Invalid Email" + matcher);
    return true;
}

private boolean shortPassword(EditText passwordField) {

    if(passwordField.getText().toString().length() > (MinPassLen-1)){
        Log.d(APP_TAG,"Valid Password");
        return false;
    }
    Log.d(APP_TAG,"Invalid Password");
    return true;
}

private void getDeviceID() {
    spAndroidID = sharedPrefs.getString(DEVICE_ID, "");

    if(spAndroidID.length() == 0) {
        // Phone has not been used before
```

```
        androidID = Secure.getString(getContentResolver(), Secure.ANDROID_ID);
        Log.d(APP_TAG,"New Shared Prefs DeviceID " + androidID);

        // ask additional security questions as it's a new phone??

        // Save AndroidID to Shared Preferences
        SharedPreferences.Editor editor = sharedPrefs.edit();
        editor.putString(DEVICE_ID, androidID);
        editor.commit();

    } else {
        // Phone has a saved deviceID
        if (spAndroidID.equals(androidID)){
            // do nothing
            Log.d(APP_TAG,"Shared Prefs DeviceID " + spAndroidID);
        } else {
            // something wrong ask additional security questions
        }
    }

    }


}
```

Take 4

In the final example, we ask the user for a username and password the first time they use the app. But this time we've encrypted the data on the server using Keyczar (see www.keyczar.org). If anyone finds the encrypted password in the shared preferences or during transmission they won't be able to decrypt it, as the encryption key is not on the phone; the password can only be decrypted by the private key, which is on the server. The downside to this is that the app needs a network connection before the user can log in.

To generate the key, take the following steps:

1. Run this command.

   ```
   java -jar KeyczarTool.jar addkey --location=./private --status=primary
   --size=4096.
   ```

2. Create a directory to contain your public key.

   ```
   mkdir public.
   ```

3. Then run this command.

   ```
   java -jar KeyczarTool.jar pubkey --location=./private --destination=./public.
   ```

Continue by following these steps:

1. Create a directory to contain your public and private key.

2. Run this command.

```
java -jar KeyczarTool.jar create --location=./private --purpose=crypt
--name="Key" --asymmetric=rsa
```

3. Run this command.

```
java -jar KeyczarTool.jar addkey --location=./private --status=primary
--size=4096
```

4. Then run this command.

```
java -jar KeyczarTool.jar pubkey --location=./private --destination=./public
to generate the public key
```

Listing 3-6 shows the client code to read the password from the activity and encrypt it with the public key for transmission back to the server.

Before we can encrypt the password using the public key we need to do the following:

1. Download AndroidKeyczarDemo from https://github.com/kruton /android-keyczar-demo.

2. Add `AndroidKeyczarReader.java` to your code.

3. Create an assets/keys folder in your project.

4. Copy in 1 and meta from the public folder where you generated the Keyczar keys.

Listing 3-6   Encrypted API Key in res/default.xml

```java
package com.riis.login;

import org.keyczar.Crypter;
import org.keyczar.exceptions.KeyczarException;
import android.os.Bundle;
import android.app.Activity;
import android.app.AlertDialog;
import android.util.Log;
import android.view.View;
import android.widget.Button;
import android.widget.EditText;


public class LoginActivity extends Activity {
```

```java
        private EditText usernameField, passwordField, emailField;
        private Button loginButton;
    private Crypter mCrypter;

    private static final String TAG = "RSADemo";

    @Override
    protected void onCreate(Bundle savedInstanceState) {
        super.onCreate(savedInstanceState);
        setContentView(R.layout.login_ screen);

        initializeViews();
        bindListenersToViews();

    }

        private void initializeViews() {
        usernameField = (EditText) findViewById(R.id.username_ field);
        passwordField = (EditText) findViewById(R.id.password_ field);
        emailField = (EditText) findViewById(R.id.email_ field);
            loginButton = (Button) findViewById(R.id.login_ button);

        }

    private void bindListenersToViews() {
        loginButton.setOnClickListener(new View.OnClickListener() {
            @Override
            public void onClick(View v) {
                    loginToApp();
            }
    });
        }

    private void loginToApp() {

                String rsaPassword = encryptPassword (passwordField.getText().
                toString());
        displaySafePassword(rsaPassword);
        // displaySafePassword(passwordField.getText().toString());
    }

        private String encryptPassword(String pass) {

                try {
                    mCrypter = new Crypter(new AndroidKeyczarReader(get
                    Resources(), "keys"));
                } catch (KeyczarException e) {
                    Log.d(TAG, "Couldn't load keyczar keys", e);
                    return null;
                }

                try {
                    final String cipherText = mCrypter.encrypt(pass);
```

```
        return cipherText;

    } catch (KeyczarException e) {
        Log.d(TAG, "Couldn't encrypt message", e);
    return null;
    }
}

private void displaySafePassword(String safePass) {
AlertDialog.Builder dialogBuilder = new AlertDialog.Builder(this);
dialogBuilder.setMessage("Password is " + safePass);
dialogBuilder.setPositiveButton("OK", null);
dialogBuilder.create().show();
}
```
}

Now that we have the encrypted API key, we send it to the server to be decrypted. The server code is in the next chapter and online at github.com/godfreynolan /bulletproof.

Application Licensing with LVL

Even though Google does not spend a huge amount of time protecting APKs from reverse engineering, they are interested in protecting apps in Google Play from being stolen by other users. It's a very common practice to pay for an app once and then side load it onto another phone or phones.

The first attempt to protect paid apps was to put all purchased apps in the /data/ app-private folder that has root-only access. But so many Android phones are rooted; it was a trivial exercise to break hiding apps in the app-private folder as a protection mechanism.

In Android 4.1 (Jelly Bean), Google introduced Google App Encryption, where paid-for applications were encrypted using a DeviceID. The theory was that paid-for apps would only run on the device where they were purchased. Unfortunately, this didn't last very long because an encrypted app's data was blown away every time the phone was rebooted, leading to a poor user experience.

Google also provides a licensing verification library (LVL) to license your app. The concept is simple—any app with the LVL library that has not been licensed will stop running.

We're not going to go into too much detail about how to use client-side LVL as it has largely been discredited. We'll see why later in this section. If you do want to add LVL to your app, you need to take the following steps:

1. Add the licensing permission to AndroidManifest.xml.

```
<uses-permission android:name="com.android.vending.CHECK _ LICENSE" />
```

2. Construct the LicenseChecker with a policy using your Google Play public key.

```
mChecker = new LicenseChecker(
        this, new ServerManagedPolicy(this,
            new AESObfuscator(SALT, getPackageName(), deviceId)),
            BASE64_PUBLIC_KEY);
```

3. Implement an obfuscator for any cached information. We're using AESObfuscator in the last step.

4. Use the `checkAccess()` LVL library call to check the license with the licensing server and deny access to the app if the license check fails (see Figure 3-2).

Sample code showing this flow can be found at https://code.google.com/p /marketlicensing/source/browse/sample/src/com/example/android/market/licensing /MainActivity.java.

The LVL license works as follows (see Figure 3-3):

1. The Android app makes a call to the Google Play app via LVL library.

2. The Google Play client collects user and device information and sends it to the server.

3. The Google License Server sees if it can match the user information against the list of people who bought the app and sends back its response to the client.

4. The Google Play client returns the results to the Android app.

5. The user is allowed to continue using the app if the license is found. If no match is found, you can then decide to tell the user to buy the app or simply exit the app.

From the last chapter we know how easy it is to decompile the app back into source code and, more importantly here, how we can use Smali to turn license checking off if we know where we're looking. It also requires you to use Google Play, which largely blocks out the Asian market that tends not to use the Google Store.

Google makes the following suggestions to improve the licensing experience for the user as well as to harden the licensing:

1. Use an obfuscator. Make sure to call the LVL library in an obfuscated class, that is, not onCreate.

2. Modify the LVL code so that it's not easy to spot.

3. Make the application tamper resistant.

4. Allow for limited amount of game play so the user will want to buy your app.

Figure 3-2   Denying access to an app using LVL

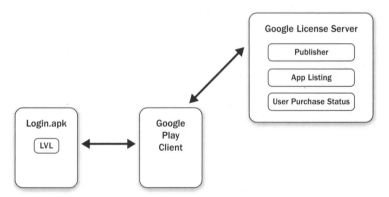

Figure 3-3   Client-side LVL

5. Try multiple background license checks if the network is down, rather than kicking the user out after the first attempt results in failure.

6. Invoke another activity, not a dialog, to inform use of validation failure.

7. Check application signature matches.

8. Make sure the app is not debuggable, as it is probably a hacked version.

9. CRC code files and compare against the original.

10. Add reflection to your license calls, noting that hackers are watching for code to packagemanager.

11. Make the license calls from the NDK, which can't be decompiled.

Listing 3-7 shows a number of these checks. But a word of warning: These checks are taken from the AntiLVL test suite. AntiLVL is an automated tool for removing license checking and can be found at http://androidcracking.blogspot.com/p /antilvl_01.html.

Listing 3-7   **AntiLVL test suite**

```
/*
 * -- IMPORTANT --
 * Please keep in mind that the code is necessarily repetitive.
 * We are using this to test AntiLVL's capacity to find instances of certain
 * codes and modify them accordingly. Code reuse optimizations would hinder
 this.
 */

package com.lohan.testtarget;

import java.io.File;
import java.lang.reflect.Method;
import java.util.HashMap;
import android.app.ProgressDialog;
import android.content.Context;
import android.content.pm.ApplicationInfo;
import android.content.pm.PackageInfo;
import android.content.pm.PackageManager;
import android.os.AsyncTask;
import android.os.Debug;

public class PerformTestsTask extends AsyncTask<Void, Void, HashMap<Integer,
TestResult>> {
    public HashMap<Integer, TestResult> myResults = new HashMap<Integer,
    TestResult>();

    Main myApp;
    ProgressDialog pd;

    // Need to update these every release
    private static final long ORIG_APK_LENGTH = 33012;
    private static final long ORIG_LAST_MODIFIED = 1319468043000L;

    // This stays the same
    private static final int SIGNATURE_HASH = 1680236448;

    PerformTestsTask(Main app) {
       myApp = app;
    }

    @Override
    protected void onPreExecute() {
       pd = ProgressDialog.show(this.myApp
```

```
                   , "Testing", "Performing tests ...", true, false, null);
        }

        @Override
        protected HashMap<Integer, TestResult> doInBackground(Void... params) {
            performChecks();
            return myResults;
        }

        @Override
        protected void onPostExecute(HashMap<Integer, TestResult> result) {
             pd.dismiss();
        }

        private void performChecks() {
            myResults.put(R.id.txtCheckDebuggerConnected_Result, checkDebugger
            Connected());
            myResults.put(R.id.txtCheckDebuggerConnectedReflection_Result, check
            DebuggerConnectedReflection());
            myResults.put(R.id.txtCheckFileLength_Result, checkFileLength());
            myResults.put(R.id.txtCheckFileLengthReflection_Result, checkFileLength
            Reflection());
            myResults.put(R.id.txtCheckLastModified_Result, checkLastModified());
            myResults.put(R.id.txtCheckLastModifiedReflection_Result, checkLast
            ModifiedReflection());
            myResults.put(R.id.txtCheckInstallerPackageName_Result, checkInstaller
            PackageName());
            myResults.put(R.id.txtCheckInstallerPackageNameReflection_Result, check
            InstallerPackageNameReflection());
            myResults.put(R.id.txtCheckPMInfoSignature_Result, checkPMInfoSignature());
            myResults.put(R.id.txtCheckPMInfoSignatureReflection_Result, checkPMInfo
            SignatureReflection());
            myResults.put(R.id.txtCheckPMCheckSignatures_Result, checkPMCheck
            Signatures());
            myResults.put(R.id.txtCheckPMCheckSignaturesReflection_Result, checkPM
            CheckSignaturesReflection());
            myResults.put(R.id.txtCheckTrivialLC1_Result, checkTrivialLicenseCheck1());
            myResults.put(R.id.txtCheckTrivialLC2_Result, checkTrivialLicenseCheck2());
            myResults.put(R.id.txtCheckDebuggable_Result, checkDebuggable());
            myResults.put(R.id.txtCheckDebuggableReflection_Result, checkDebuggable
            Reflection());
        }

        private TestResult checkDebuggerConnected() {
            boolean debugConn = Debug.isDebuggerConnected();

            Console.log("checkDebuggerConnected() = " + debugConn);

            if ( debugConn )
                return TestResult.FAILED;
            else
                return TestResult.PASSED;
        }

        private TestResult checkDebuggerConnectedReflection() {
            boolean debugConn;
            Method m = null;
```

```
        try {
            m = Debug.class.getMethod("isDebuggerConnected");
            debugConn = (Boolean) m.invoke(null);
        } catch (Exception e) {
            e.printStackTrace();
            return TestResult.ERROR;
        }

        Console.log("checkDebuggerConnectedReflection() = " + debugConn);

        if ( debugConn )
            return TestResult.FAILED;
        else
            return TestResult.PASSED;
    }

    private TestResult checkFileLength() {
        String path = Main.MyContext.getPackageCodePath();
        File f = new File(path);
        Long val = null;

        try {
            val = f.length();
            Console.log("package code path: " + path + " size: " + val);
        } catch (Exception e) {
            e.printStackTrace();
            return TestResult.ERROR;
        }

        Console.log("checkFileSize() = " + val + "  compare:" + (ORIG_APK_LENGTH
        + 20));

        if ( val != null && val <= ORIG_APK_LENGTH + 30 )
            return TestResult.PASSED;
        else
            return TestResult.FAILED;
    }

    private TestResult checkFileLengthReflection() {
        String path = Main.MyContext.getPackageCodePath();
        File f = new File(path);
        Long val = null;
        Method m = null;
        try {
            m = File.class.getMethod("length", new Class[] {});
            val = (Long) m.invoke(f);
        } catch (Exception e) {
            e.printStackTrace();
            return TestResult.ERROR;
        }

        Console.log("checkFileSizeReflection() = " + val + "  compare:" + (ORIG_
        APK_LENGTH + 20));

        if ( val != null && val <= ORIG_APK_LENGTH + 20 )
            return TestResult.PASSED;
        else
```

```
            return TestResult.FAILED;
}

private TestResult checkLastModified() {
    String path = Main.MyContext.getPackageCodePath();
    File f = new File(path);
    Long val = null;

    try {
        val = f.lastModified();
    } catch (Exception e) {
        e.printStackTrace();
        return TestResult.ERROR;
    }

    Console.log("checkLastModified() = " + val + " compare:" + (ORIG_LAST_
    MODIFIED + 120000));

    // two minute grace period since i wont actually know modified time
    // until it's last modified and i'll have to update it again afterwards.
    if ( val != null && val <= ORIG_LAST_MODIFIED + 120000 )
        return TestResult.PASSED;
    else
        return TestResult.FAILED;
}

private TestResult checkLastModifiedReflection() {
    String path = Main.MyContext.getPackageCodePath();
    File f = new File(path);
    Long val = null;
    Method m = null;
    try {
        m = File.class.getMethod("lastModified", new Class[] {});
        val = (Long) m.invoke(f);
    } catch (Exception e) {
        e.printStackTrace();
        return TestResult.ERROR;
    }

    Console.log("checkLastModifiedReflection() = " + val + " compare:" +
    (ORIG_LAST_MODIFIED + 120000));

    if ( val != null && val <= ORIG_LAST_MODIFIED + 120000 )
        return TestResult.PASSED;
    else
        return TestResult.FAILED;
}

private TestResult checkInstallerPackageName() {
    String ipName = null;
    try {
        ipName = Main.MyPM.getInstallerPackageName(Main.MyPackageName);

        Console.log("checkInstallerPackageName() = " + ipName);
    } catch (Exception e) {
        e.printStackTrace();
        return TestResult.ERROR;
```

```
    }

    // com.google.android.feedback
    if (ipName != null && ipName.contains("oid.fe"))
        return TestResult.PASSED;
    else
        return TestResult.FAILED;
}

private TestResult checkInstallerPackageNameReflection() {
    String ipName = "";
    try {
        Method m = PackageManager.class.getMethod(
                "getInstallerPackageName", new Class[] { String.class });
        ipName = (String) m.invoke(Main.MyPM, new Object[] { Main.MyPackage
        Name });
        Console.log("checkInstallerPackageNameReflection() = " + ipName);

    } catch (Exception e) {
        e.printStackTrace();
        return TestResult.ERROR;
    }

    // google.android.feedback
    if (ipName != null && ipName.contains("oid.fe"))
        return TestResult.PASSED;
    else
        return TestResult.FAILED;
}

private TestResult checkPMInfoSignature() {
    PackageInfo pi = null;
    try {
        pi = Main.MyPM.getPackageInfo(Main.MyPackageName, PackageManager.
        GET_SIGNATURES);
    } catch (Exception e) {
        e.printStackTrace();
        return TestResult.ERROR;
    }

    int sigHash = pi.signatures[0].hashCode();
    Console.log("checkPMInfoSignature() = " + sigHash + " compare:" +
SIGNATURE_HASH);

    if ( sigHash == SIGNATURE_HASH )
        return TestResult.PASSED;
    else
        return TestResult.FAILED;
}

private TestResult checkPMInfoSignatureReflection() {
    int sigHash;
    try {
        Method m = PackageManager.class.getMethod("getPackageInfo",
                new Class[] { String.class, int.class });
        PackageInfo pi = (PackageInfo) m.invoke(Main.MyPM, new Object[] {
                Main.MyPackageName, PackageManager.GET_SIGNATURES });
```

```
            sigHash = pi.signatures[0].hashCode();
        } catch (Exception e) {
            e.printStackTrace();
            return TestResult.ERROR;
        }

        Console.log("checkPMInfoSignatureReflection() = " + sigHash + " compare:" +
        SIGNATURE_HASH);

        if ( sigHash == SIGNATURE_HASH )
            return TestResult.PASSED;
        else
            return TestResult.FAILED;
    }

    private TestResult checkPMCheckSignatures() {
        int res = PackageManager.SIGNATURE_NO_MATCH;
        try {
            res = Main.MyPM.checkSignatures(Main.MyPackageName, "com.android.
            phone");
        } catch (Exception e) {
            e.printStackTrace();
            return TestResult.ERROR;
        }

        Console.log("checkPMCheckSignatures() = " + res);

        if ( res == PackageManager.SIGNATURE_MATCH )
            return TestResult.PASSED;
        else
            return TestResult.FAILED;
    }

    private TestResult checkPMCheckSignaturesReflection() {
        Integer res = PackageManager.SIGNATURE_NO_MATCH;
        try {
            Method m = PackageManager.class.getMethod("checkSignatures",
                    new Class[] { String.class, String.class });
            // this should give a failure
            res = (Integer) m.invoke(Main.MyPM, new Object[] {
                    Main.MyPackageName, "com.android.vending" });
        } catch (Exception e) {
            e.printStackTrace();
            return TestResult.ERROR;
        }

        Console.log("checkPMCheckSignaturesReflection() = " + res);

        if ( res == PackageManager.SIGNATURE_MATCH )
            return TestResult.PASSED;
        else
            return TestResult.FAILED;
    }

    private TestResult checkTrivialLicenseCheck1() {
        if ( TrivialLicenseCheck.isValidLicense() && TrivialLicenseCheck.isApp
        Licensed()
```

```
                    && TrivialLicenseCheck.publicHasUserDonated() )
            return TestResult.PASSED;
        else
            return TestResult.FAILED;
    }

    private TestResult checkTrivialLicenseCheck2() {
        if ( TrivialLicenseCheck.isAuthed() )
            return TestResult.PASSED;
        else
            return TestResult.FAILED;
    }

    private TestResult checkDebuggable() {
        ApplicationInfo ai = Main.MyContext.getApplicationInfo();
        boolean isDebuggable = (0 != (ai.flags &=
            ApplicationInfo.FLAG_DEBUGGABLE));

        Console.log("checkDebuggable() flags = " + ai.flags);

        if ( isDebuggable )
            return TestResult.FAILED;
        else
            return TestResult.PASSED;
    }

    private TestResult checkDebuggableReflection() {
        ApplicationInfo ai = null;
        try {
            Method m = Context.class.getMethod("getApplicationInfo");
            ai = (ApplicationInfo) m.invoke(Main.MyContext);
        } catch (Exception e) {
            e.printStackTrace();
            return TestResult.ERROR;
        }

        Console.log("checkDebuggableReflection() flags = " + ai.flags);

        boolean isDebuggable = (0 != (ai.flags &=
            ApplicationInfo.FLAG_DEBUGGABLE));

        if ( isDebuggable )
            return TestResult.FAILED;
        else
            return TestResult.PASSED;
    }
}
```

In Listing 3-8 we show some decompiled LicenseCheck code from an LVL-protected APK. The original APK comes from the http://hackplayers.com website, which challenged people to remove the licensing.

It should be obvious from the LicenseChecker call on line 43 where the call is being made and how it can be removed. In this case it would be straightforward enough to alter the code, recompile, and resign. However, in most cases the LicenseChecker call would be commented out in a Smali file, then reassembled and resigned.

Listing 3-8   **Decompiled LVL code**

```
package com.hpys.crackmes;

import android.app.Activity;
import android.app.AlertDialog.Builder;
import android.app.Dialog;
import android.content.DialogInterface;
import android.content.DialogInterface.OnClickListener;
import android.content.Intent;
import android.content.pm.ApplicationInfo;
import android.net.Uri;
import android.os.Bundle;
import android.provider.Settings.Secure;
import android.widget.Toast;
import com.android.vending.licensing.AESObfuscator;
import com.android.vending.licensing.LicenseChecker;
import com.android.vending.licensing.LicenseCheckerCallback;
import com.android.vending.licensing.LicenseCheckerCallback.ApplicationErrorCode;
import com.android.vending.licensing.ServerManagedPolicy;

public class LicenseCheck extends Activity
{
  private static final String BASE64_PUBLIC_KEY = "MIGfMA0GCSqGSIb3DQEBAQUAA4GNA
DCBiQKBgQCySptbugHAzWUJY3ALWhuSCPhVXnwbUBfsRExYQitBCVny4V1DcU2SAx22bH9dSM0X7NdMObF
74r+Wd77QoPAtaySqFLqCeRCbFmhHgVSi+pGeCipTpueefSkz2AX8Aj+9x27tqjBsX1LtNWVLDsinEhBWN
68R+iEOmf/6jGWObQIDAQAB";
  private static final byte[] SALT = { 45, 77, 117, 36, 12, 89, 29, 18, 37, 7, 113,
  11, 32, -64, 89, 72, -94, 51, 88, 95 };
  private LicenseChecker mChecker;
  private LicenseCheckerCallback mLicenseCheckerCallback;

  private void doCheck()
  {
    this.mChecker.checkAccess(this.mLicenseCheckerCallback);
  }

  private void startMainActivity()
  {
    startActivity(new Intent(this, MyAndroidAppActivity.class));
    finish();
  }

  public void onCreate(Bundle paramBundle)
  {
    super.onCreate(paramBundle);
    String str = Settings.Secure.getString(getContentResolver(), "android_id");
    this.mLicenseCheckerCallback = new MyLicenseCheckerCallback(null); // line 42
```

```
    this.mChecker = new LicenseChecker(this, new ServerManagedPolicy(this, new
AESObfuscator(SALT, getPackageName(), str)), "MIGfMA0GCSqGSIb3DQEBAQUAA4GNADCBiQKBg
QCySptbugHAzWUJY3ALWhuSCPhVXnwbUBfsRExYQitBCVny4V1DcU2SAx22bH9dSM0X7NdMObF74r+Wd77
QoPAtaySqFLqCeRCbFmhHgVSi+pGeCipTpueefSkz2AX8Aj+9x27tqjBsX1LtNWVLDsinEhBWN68R+iEOm
f/6jGWObQIDAQAB");
    doCheck();
}

protected Dialog onCreateDialog(int paramInt)
{
    return new AlertDialog.Builder(this).setTitle("Application Not Licensed").
    setCancelable(false).setMessage("This application is not licensed. Please
    purchase it from Android Market").setPositiveButton("Buy App", new Dialog
    Interface.OnClickListener()
    {
      public void onClick(DialogInterface paramAnonymousDialogInterface, int
      paramAnonymousInt)
      {
        Intent localIntent = new Intent("android.intent.action.VIEW", Uri.parse
        ("http://market.android.com/details?id=" + LicenseCheck.this.getPackage
        Name()));
        LicenseCheck.this.startActivity(localIntent);
        LicenseCheck.this.finish();
      }
    }).setNegativeButton("Exit", new DialogInterface.OnClickListener()
    {
      public void onClick(DialogInterface paramAnonymousDialogInterface, int
      paramAnonymousInt)
      {
        LicenseCheck.this.finish();
      }
    }).create();
}

protected void onDestroy()
{
  super.onDestroy();
  this.mChecker.onDestroy();
}

public void toast(String paramString)
{
  Toast.makeText(this, paramString, 0).show();
}

private class MyLicenseCheckerCallback
  implements LicenseCheckerCallback
{
  private MyLicenseCheckerCallback()
  {
  }

  public void allow()
  {
    LicenseCheck.this.setContentView(2130903040);
    if (LicenseCheck.this.isFinishing())
      return;
```

```
      ApplicationInfo localApplicationInfo = LicenseCheck.this.getApplication
Info();
      int i = 0x2 & localApplicationInfo.flags;
      localApplicationInfo.flags = i;
      if (i != 0);
      for (int j = 1; ; j = 0)
      {
        if (j != 0)
          dontAllow();
        LicenseCheck.this.startMainActivity();
        return;
      }
    }

    public void applicationError(LicenseCheckerCallback.ApplicationErrorCode
paramApplicationErrorCode)
    {
      if (LicenseCheck.this.isFinishing())
        return;
      LicenseCheck.this.toast("Error: " + paramApplicationErrorCode.name());
      LicenseCheck.this.startMainActivity();
    }

    public void dontAllow()
    {
      if (LicenseCheck.this.isFinishing())
        return;
      LicenseCheck.this.showDialog(0);
    }
  }
}
```

Given what we've seen, client-side LVL is more likely to frustrate your paying users than keep someone from stealing your app. It is possible to move the LVL checking to your server instead of the client. Access is then granted to the client side via a session token. Google provides some sample code here, which would be the recommended approach unless the client-side LVL changes in the future: https://code.google.com /p/marketlicensing/source/browse/library/src/com/android/vending/licensing /LicenseValidator.java.

OAuth

As you get further into the security aspects of Android security and the thought of creating your own session management system seems like too much overhead, you might want to think about using someone else's authentication mechanism using OAuth.

OAuth has been around in one form or another since 2006. Many of the major Internet apps of the last decade support OAuth, including Facebook, Dropbox, 37signals, GitHub, and many others.

Potentially, this approach could remove the need to store usernames and passwords locally, and you could simply leverage someone else's authentication to allow someone to log in to your app. This would be ideal from our point of view as we wouldn't have to worry about managing usernames and passwords anymore. But, in reality, OAuth is probably going to be used as an alternative rather than as a replacement to your existing login mechanism.

We're going to look at using Facebook's OAuth implementation. Other implementations with the other websites mentioned above will be similar.

OAuth with Facebook

In this OAuth example we'll provide the option to allow the user to log in and control the session length via Facebook.

So how do we do this? Just follow these steps:

1. Download the Facebook APK from developers.facebook.com and install it on the emulator.

2. Next we need to create the app in Facebook. We do that by choosing Developers Settings or going to Apps->Create New App.

3. Create the Bulletproof Android app and choose a category (see Figure 3-4).

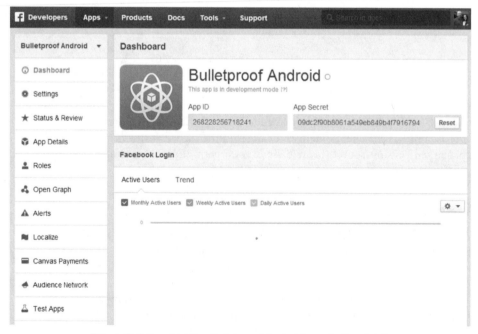

Figure 3-4 Creating the Bulletproof Android app in Facebook

4. Click on Settings and Add Platform and chose Android as your platform.

5. Facebook requires a hash key for the machine that the app is created on using the Java keytool command.

6. To run the following command you're also going to need to have openssl installed on your machine, which is available from http://openssl.org. In this example, openssl is installed in the c:\adt directory.

```
keytool -exportcert -alias androiddebugkey -keystore %HOMEPATH%\.android
\debug.keystore | openssl sha1 -binary | openssl base64
```

7. Enter the default keystore password, which is "android".

   a. Enter keystore password: android

   b. Hashkey: ctoMkOd56ExXvPSjvf3mKNopmiE=

8. Add the hashkey into the Facebook app web page (see Figure 3-5).

9. Using our simple login app and the template code that comes from the developer.facebook.com website, we insert the App ID (see line 20 in Listing 3-9).

10. Now run the app and log in by clicking on the new Login to Facebook button (see Figure 3-6).

Template code for logging in with Facebook is shown in Listing 3-9.

Listing 3-9 **Login using Facebook**

```
package com.riis.facebookintegration;

import org.json.JSONObject;

import com.facebook.android.DialogError;
import com.facebook.android.Facebook;
import com.facebook.android.FacebookError;
import com.facebook.android.Facebook.DialogListener;
import com.facebook.android.Util;

import android.app.Activity;
import android.content.Intent;
import android.os.Bundle;
import android.view.View;
import android.view.View.OnClickListener;
import android.widget.Button;
import android.widget.Toast;

public class Login extends Activity {

    public static final String mAPP_ID = "268228256718241";   // line 20
    public Facebook mFacebook = new Facebook(mAPP_ID);

    @Override
```

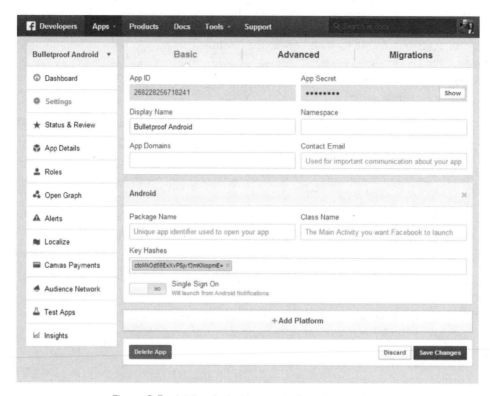

Figure 3-5   Adding Android as a platform for your app

Figure 3-6   Login screen with Facebook button

```java
public void onCreate(Bundle savedInstanceState) {
    super.onCreate(savedInstanceState);
    setContentView(R.layout.main);
    ((Button)findViewById(R.id.LoginButton)).setOnClickListener( loginButton
    Listener );
    SessionStore.restore(mFacebook, this);
    }

@Override
protected void onActivityResult(int requestCode, int resultCode, Intent data)
{
    mFacebook.authorizeCallback(requestCode, resultCode, data);
    }


private OnClickListener loginButtonListener = new OnClickListener() {
    public void onClick( View v ) {
        if( !mFacebook.isSessionValid() ) {
            Toast.makeText(Login.this, "Authorizing", Toast.LENGTH_SHORT).
            show();
            mFacebook.authorize(Login.this, new String[] { "" }, new Login
            DialogListener());
            }
        else {
            Toast.makeText( Login.this, "Has valid session", Toast.LENGTH_
            SHORT).show();
            try {
                JSONObject json = Util.parseJson(mFacebook.request("me"));
                String facebookID = json.getString("id");
                String firstName = json.getString("first_name");
                String lastName = json.getString("last_name");
                Toast.makeText(Login.this, "You already have a valid session,
                " + firstName + " " + lastName + ". No need to re-
                authorize.", Toast.LENGTH_SHORT).show();
                }
            catch( Exception error ) {
                Toast.makeText( Login.this, error.toString(), Toast.LENGTH_
                SHORT).show();
                }
            catch( FacebookError error ) {
                Toast.makeText( Login.this, error.toString(), Toast.LENGTH_
                SHORT).show();
                }
            }
        }
    };

public final class LoginDialogListener implements DialogListener {
    public void onComplete(Bundle values) {
        try {

            JSONObject json = Util.parseJson(mFacebook.request("me"));
            String facebookID = json.getString("id");
            String firstName = json.getString("first_name");
            String lastName = json.getString("last_name");
```

```
                    Toast.makeText( Login.this, "Thank you for Logging In, " + first
                    Name + " " + lastName + "!", Toast.LENGTH _ LONG).show();
                    SessionStore.save(mFacebook, Login.this);
                    }
                catch( Exception error ) {
                    Toast.makeText( Login.this, error.toString(), Toast.LENGTH _ SHORT).
                    show();
                    }
                catch( FacebookError error ) {
                    Toast.makeText( Login.this, error.toString(), Toast.LENGTH _ SHORT).
                    show();
                    }
                }

        public void onFacebookError(FacebookError error) {
            Toast.makeText( Login.this, "Something went wrong. Please try again.",
            Toast.LENGTH _ LONG).show();
            }

        public void onError(DialogError error) {
            Toast.makeText( Login.this, "Something went wrong. Please try again.",
            Toast.LENGTH _ LONG).show();
            }

         public void onCancel() {
            Toast.makeText( Login.this, "Something went wrong. Please try again.",
            Toast.LENGTH _ LONG).show();
            }
        }


    }
```

Web and Mobile Session Management

The length of a web browser session varies from website to website, but the default is
typically 30 minutes. For usability reasons the default for mobile apps is much longer.
A mobile user would not expect to have to log in to the same app more than once or,
at most, twice a day. Most apps allow the user to remain logged in for days at a time.

The lifecycle of an Android app means that it can go into the background and be
restarted as long as the user doesn't intentionally stop it by removing it from the list of
active apps.

There seems to be a perception that mobile apps should allow you to stay logged
in permanently, but this isn't secure. Choose a reasonable session timeout for your
Android app. If it's a financial or healthcare app, the session should be minutes from
the last activity. If it's a game, the session can be days.

If the app is authenticated using OAuth, then there is another session that needs
to be managed outside of the Android lifecycle. When the user logs in to the app, a
username and password are sent to an API that checks login credentials for validity and
returns a session token.

The token is then used for any future API calls until the token or session is revoked.

We'll need to revoke tokens under the following conditions:

- If the phone is stolen
- When we need the user to update for a new security patch and log in again
- When the user doesn't have a lock on the phone
- When making a credit card payment or other financial transaction
- When the user is changing a password or other profile information

If a device is lost or stolen, in a best-case scenario whoever has the phone should not be able to log in to apps with any personal information. If the phone wasn't locked, then ideally the sessions should have timed out so that the person with the phone will be required to log in. For this reason, tokens should expire each day or two so that the user has to log in again. You may also want to ask the user to re-enter their app password when changing any settings so that a casual user cannot change a password.

Some apps ask a user to enter a username and password again when they start a financial transaction, for example, when paying for something with a credit card. This way, someone cannot just pick up the phone and create a bogus transaction without needing to enter a username and password.

More template Facebook code is shown in Listing 3-10, where we've modified the code to set the expiration time to thirty minutes (see line 30) rather than never expiring the tokens. Finally, make sure you log in over HTTPS, otherwise you're giving away your login credentials to both your app and Facebook.

Listing 3-10 **Setting the expiration time**

```
package com.riis.facebookintegration;

import com.facebook.android.Facebook;
import android.content.Context;
import android.content.SharedPreferences;
import android.content.SharedPreferences.Editor;

public class SessionStore {

    private static final String TOKEN = "access_token";
    private static final String EXPIRES = "expires_in";
    private static final String KEY = "facebook-session";
    private static final Integer THIRTY_MIN = 1800000;


    public static boolean save(Facebook session, Context context) {
        Editor editor =
            context.getSharedPreferences(KEY, Context.MODE_PRIVATE).edit();
        editor.putString(TOKEN, session.getAccessToken());
        editor.putLong(EXPIRES, session.getAccessExpires());
        return editor.commit();
    }
```

```
public static boolean restore(Facebook session, Context context) {
    SharedPreferences savedSession =
        context.getSharedPreferences(KEY, Context.MODE_PRIVATE);
    session.setAccessToken(savedSession.getString(TOKEN, null));
    session.setAccessExpires(savedSession.getLong(EXPIRES, System.
    currentTimeMillis()+THIRTY_MIN));                    // line 30
    return session.isSessionValid();
}

public static void clear(Context context) {
    Editor editor =
        context.getSharedPreferences(KEY, Context.MODE_PRIVATE).edit();
    editor.clear();
    editor.commit();
}
```

}

Vulnerability

Note that we are also saving our token in shared preferences in Listing 3-10. It's important that this is not seen, otherwise someone can impersonate you on Facebook. Some recent articles reveal just how dangerous this can be—see http://thehackernews.com/2014/07/facebook-sdk-vulnerability-puts.html.

In the next chapter we'll look at how to hide API keys using public/private keys, which can also be used with Facebook access tokens.

User Behavior

In December 2010, the gossip site Gawker was hacked and the entire database of 1.3 million users was pushed up on a number of BitTorrent websites along with the Gawker source code. The passwords weren't in cleartext, but they had been hashed. However, hashed password files can be broken using a brute-force dictionary attack, so 400,000 usernames and passwords were quickly found.

Fast forward to a couple of years later, when we ran the same database of usernames and passwords against a completely different website. It's common knowledge that lots of people use the same username and password on multiple sites because they don't want to juggle different logins for different websites. Sixty thousand of the 400,000 hacked usernames and passwords were the same two years later on a completely different website.

Our client created temporary passwords for the 60,000 users and asked them to reset their password when they next logged in.

So next time you log into your favorite app and it asks you to reset your password, you know that's probably because of a website that has been hacked and has matching usernames and passwords

A good way to start testing logins on your Android app is to use Calabash (see http://calaba.sh), which is Cucumber for Android.

Listing 3-11 shows a simple table-driven Calabash script to run some table-driven username and password combinations. And if some of the Gawker usernames and passwords turn up in your file, then you should reset the passwords and send the user a temporary password.

To run the Calabash scripts, take the following steps:

1. Install Ruby and Calabash.

2. Start Android emulator.

3. Install the APK on the emulator.

   ```
   adb -s emulator-5554 install com.riis.login-1.apk
   ```

4. Run the tests.

   ```
   calabash-android run com.riis.login-1.apk
   ```

Listing 3-11 **Calabash script**

```
Scenario Outline:  Invalid Login
  Given I am on the Login screen
    When I enter "<username>" into the username field
    And I enter "<password>" into the password field
    And I press the "Done" button
    And I press the "OK" button

Examples:
  | username                    | password |
  | martha@executivelamps.info  | 123456   |
  | santa@northpole.org         | password |
  | jenkins@tdd.org             | letmein  |
  | last@email.com              | iloveyou |
```

Two (or More) Factor Authentication

At the time of this writing, the *New York Times* is reporting that a small Russian team of hackers has compromised 1.2 billion usernames and passwords. This news comes less than six months since the last major hack that exposed millions of passwords, the SSL Heartbleed attack. Although the 1.2 billion usernames and passwords from the Russian hack aren't readily available, you have to ask yourself, "Is the system of using usernames and passwords broken beyond repair?"

Many websites are moving to a two or more factor authentication where in order to log into the app you need to enter a one-time code from an SMS message or a SecurID token. To date there really aren't many two-factor authentication mobile apps because both take place on the same phone, which isn't a good idea if someone already has access to your phone.

Conclusion

In this chapter we looked at how developers have tried to secure usernames and passwords with varying degrees of success. We also covered how to use Keyczar to create a more robust authentication mechanism. We looked at Android licensing and how it has been cracked. We looked at OAuth and how to use Facebook as a third-party login mechanism. We finished with some discussion on how mobile behavior can crack even the most secure systems, through no fault of your own, and what you can do to combat this.

4

Network Communication

In this chapter we look at how to encrypt data and how to send information securely across the network using SSL. We also look at how hackers might perform a man-in-the-middle (MITM) attack using an SSL proxy, which intercepts the communication to see whether it's really secure. In Chapter 2 we talked about the pros and cons of storing any sensitive data on the phone or tablet; generally, it's not a good idea and should be avoided if possible. A better solution is to store the data remotely where it's away from prying eyes.

However, when you send the data to a remote server you have to be careful that it's encrypted when you are sending it. This could be done using SSL, and you can also encrypt it on one end yourself and then decrypt it at the server. There are plenty of cryptographic libraries in Android that enable you to encrypt the information before transmission. But the problem with encrypting data is that we have to be very careful to not fool ourselves into thinking that the information is secure, and that we are sending it where we think we're sending it.

In modern browsers, if you connect via secure HTTP, or HTTPS, over a secure sockets layer you'll get a little green or gold lock showing that you're in a secure encrypted transaction. Developers pay a Certificate Authority (CA) to make sure that they are who they say they are. And if you happen to come across a site that isn't a valid site, your web browser will alert you pretty quickly that something is wrong. Unfortunately, there isn't anything similar in mobile computing—there is no lock or key to comfort the user that any and all network communication is encrypted. There is a chance that a third party, a man in the middle, sitting between you and the server is trying to decrypt your sensitive information. We'll show you how to be sure that won't be an issue for your app.

And what exactly do we mean by "sensitive data"? Well, this varies by the type of application. It can be bank or credit card information, social security numbers, or payroll information. It can be usernames and passwords that might allow someone to impersonate the user at a later time within the app or on a website. If it's a healthcare app that needs to be HIPAA compliant, then it's anything that identifies a patient, which can be as simple as a name or address.

Like we do throughout this book, we're going to show how developers have tried to send data across the network, with each example hopefully getting more and more secure. The outline for this chapter is as follows:

1. HTTP call with API key

2. HTTPS call with API key

3. Symmetric encryption and attempts at hiding the key

4. Asymmetric encryption or public/private API key exchange

5. Man-in-the-middle attack using Charles Proxy

HTTP(S) Connection

API providers use API keys as a simple authentication mechanism so they can charge for their data, whether that's traffic information, stock market data, or weather information. Figure 4-1 shows a simple app that allows us to call a Weather Underground URL to display the current weather conditions for your area. In the app, you can either send the request via HTTP or HTTPS by clicking the appropriate button.

If you're sending the request via HTTP or HTTPS the URL is called as follows, where 2ee858dd063ef50e is the API key:

http(s)://api.wunderground.com/api/2ee858dd063ef50e/conditions/q/MI/Troy.json

The response is parsed and the weather shown for Troy, MI (see Figure 4-2). Feel free to enter your own API key or play around with the code. See Listing 4-1 to change the city and state.

Although there are plenty of similar APIs out there, Weather Underground is useful for our purposes because it requires your own API key to retrieve data, so we have to think about how to protect our API.

Listing 4-1   **HTTP(S) calls to Weather Underground**

```
package com.riis.restfulwebservice;

import java.io.BufferedReader;
import java.io.InputStreamReader;

import org.apache.http.HttpResponse;
import org.apache.http.client.methods.HttpGet;
import org.apache.http.impl.client.DefaultHttpClient;
import org.apache.http.protocol.BasicHttpContext;
```

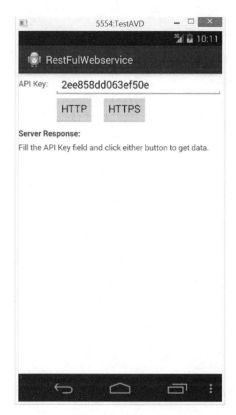

Figure 4-1   Android client request

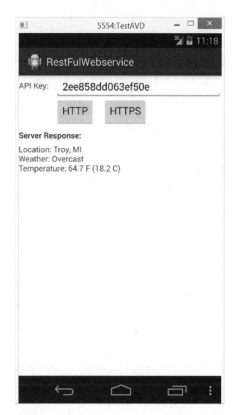

Figure 4-2   Android client response

```
import org.json.JSONObject;

import com.riis.restfulwebservice.R;

import android.os.AsyncTask;
import android.os.Bundle;
import android.app.Activity;
import android.app.ProgressDialog;
import android.view.View;
import android.view.View.OnClickListener;
import android.widget.Button;
import android.widget.EditText;
import android.widget.TextView;

public class RestFulWebservice extends Activity {

    final String URL1 = "api.wunderground.com/api/";
    final String URL2 = "/conditions/q/MI/Troy.json";
```

```java
@Override
public void onCreate(Bundle savedInstanceState) {
    super.onCreate(savedInstanceState);
    setContentView(R.layout.rest_ful_webservice);
    final Button HTTP = (Button) findViewById(R.id.HTTP);
    HTTP.setOnClickListener(new OnClickListener() {
    @Override
    public void onClick(View arg0) {
        new HTTPCall().execute("http://" + URL1 + ((EditText) findViewById(R.
        id.api)).getText().toString() + URL2);
    }
    });
    final Button HTTPS = (Button) findViewById(R.id.HTTPS);
    HTTPS.setOnClickListener(new OnClickListener() {
    @Override
    public void onClick(View arg0) {
        new HTTPCall().execute("https://" + URL1 + ((EditText) findViewById(R.
        id.api)).getText().toString() + URL2);
    }
    });
}

private class HTTPCall  extends AsyncTask<String, Void, Void> {

    private ProgressDialog dialog = new ProgressDialog(RestFulWebservice.
    this);
    String responseData = "";

    protected void onPreExecute() {
        dialog.setMessage("Please wait..");
        dialog.show();
        ((TextView) findViewById(R.id.output)).setText("");
    }

    protected Void doInBackground(String... urls) {
    try {
      HttpResponse response = (new DefaultHttpClient()).execute((new HttpGet
      (urls[0])), (new BasicHttpContext()));
      StringBuilder builder = new StringBuilder();
      BufferedReader reader = new BufferedReader(new InputStreamReader
      (response.getEntity().getContent()));
      String line;
      while((line = reader.readLine()) != null) {
        builder.append(line);
      }
      responseData = builder.toString();
      response.getEntity().consumeContent();
    } catch (Exception ex) {
      responseData = ex.getMessage();
      ex.printStackTrace();
    }
    return null;
    }

    protected void onPostExecute(Void unused) {
      try {
```

```
    JSONObject observation = new JSONObject(responseData).getJSONObject
    ("current_observation");
    String result = "";
result += "Location: " + observation.getJSONObject("display_location").
getString("full") + "\n";
result += "Weather: " + observation.getString("weather") + "\n";
result += "Temperature: " + observation.getString("temperature_
string");
        ((TextView) findViewById(R.id.output)).setText(result);
} catch (Exception ex) {
        ((TextView) findViewById(R.id.output)).setText(responseData);
    ex.printStackTrace();
}

    dialog.dismiss();
    }
    }
}
```

An app can make up to 500 free calls per day to the Weather Underground API. But if the weather app becomes relatively successful, then 5000 calls per day costs $20/month. Based on the number of downloads and number of API calls you're seeing, that seems like it will be enough for you. But if one or more people decompile your APK, find your API key, and then start using it in their own apps, then 5000 calls per day suddenly doesn't seem like all that much anymore. Worse still, you app stops working as you're going over 5000 calls on a regular basis because now it's no longer just your users making the calls.

In Figure 4-3 we're showing the traffic to the Weather Underground for both the HTTP and HTTPS calls using a tool called Charles Proxy. You'll learn how to set this

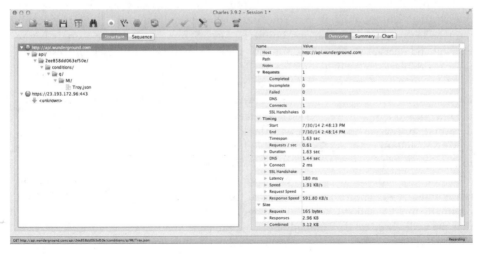

Figure 4-3   Charles Proxy

up later in the chapter, but it should be obvious from the screenshot that if your call is made via HTTP, your API key is going to be visible to anyone who cares to look. Things look better if we send it via HTTPS.

In a real app we would need to hide the API key somewhere in the APK and hope that it wouldn't be found. If your API key is compromised you'll need to regenerate it. Your existing users will then have to update your app to get it working again. The consequences to this can annoy your users enough that they might uninstall, which can have some effects downstream depending on how you measure your stats.

Symmetric Keys

To keep our weather underground API key secure, we'll need a place to hide it. In Chapter 5 we'll discover how developers have tried to hide passwords with varying degrees of success, as follows:

1. Ask for the password each time.

2. Save it in cleartext in shared preferences.

3. Save it encrypted in shared preferences using a one-time key.

4. Save it encrypted in the shared preferences using a device-specific key.

5. Hide it in the NDK.

Many of these same techniques apply here, but because we don't want to cover the same information twice, we won't go into too much detail until Chapter 5.

There are a number of choices open to you on how you want to encrypt data on an Android phone, and many different cryptographic libraries are available to encrypt the data depending on the phone. Your initial choice should probably begin by deciding whether to use symmetric or asymmetric keys. Symmetric keys use a single key to encrypt and decrypt the data. Asymmetric keys use public and private keys to share information between a client and a server.

Most of the apps that we've audited are using a single symmetric encryption key for every user. The problem with this approach is that we have to find a place to hide the encryption key. But we've seen a number of times already just how easy it is to decompile or reverse engineer an APK back into source code, so it's really only a matter of time before someone finds the key. If it's a symmetric key, then that can be used to decrypt the API key and we're back to where we started.

Listing 4-2 shows some sample encryption and decryption code using AES, which is a symmetric key algorithm. It was taken from a well-known airline's app and was originally in a file called Crypto.java, suggesting that the developers were not aware that the code could be decompiled. Compile the code and run the code as `java SimpleTest`. The airline app has since been updated and now uses a device-specific key, but unfortunately that only means we have to copy and paste another couple lines of code into our SimpleTest file to generate the new key. We also have to run the code on the target device.

Listing 4-2 **Symmetric key encryption/decryption**

```java
import java.security.SecureRandom;
import javax.crypto.Cipher;
import javax.crypto.KeyGenerator;
import javax.crypto.SecretKey;
import javax.crypto.spec.SecretKeySpec;

public class SimpleTest {

    public static void main(String[] args) {
        try {
            String plaintext = "1234", key = "3lIoM_d0idrn4|4TleD";
            String ciphertext = encrypt(key, plaintext);
            String plaintext2 = decrypt(key, ciphertext);
            System.out.println("Encrypting '" + plaintext +
                            "' yields: (" + ciphertext.length() + ") " + ciphertext);
            System.out.println("Decrypting it yields: " + plaintext2);
        }
        catch (Exception ex) {
            ex.printStackTrace();
        }
    }

    public static String encrypt(String seed, String cleartext) throws Exception {
        byte[] rawKey = getRawKey(seed.getBytes());
        byte[] result = encrypt(rawKey, cleartext.getBytes());
        return toHex(result);
    }

    public static String decrypt(String seed, String encrypted) throws Exception {
        byte[] rawKey = getRawKey(seed.getBytes());
        byte[] enc = toByte(encrypted);
        byte[] result = decrypt(rawKey, enc);
        return new String(result);
    }

    private static byte[] getRawKey(byte[] seed) throws Exception {
        KeyGenerator kgen = KeyGenerator.getInstance("AES");
        SecureRandom sr = SecureRandom.getInstance("SHA1PRNG");
        sr.setSeed(seed);
        kgen.init(128, sr); // 192 and 256 bits may not be available
        SecretKey skey = kgen.generateKey();
        byte[] raw = skey.getEncoded();
        return raw;
    }


    private static byte[] encrypt(byte[] raw, byte[] clear) throws Exception {
        SecretKeySpec skeySpec = new SecretKeySpec(raw, "AES");
        Cipher cipher = Cipher.getInstance("AES");
        cipher.init(Cipher.ENCRYPT_MODE, skeySpec);
```

```
        byte[] encrypted = cipher.doFinal(clear);
        return encrypted;
    }

    private static byte[] decrypt(byte[] raw, byte[] encrypted) throws Exception {
        SecretKeySpec skeySpec = new SecretKeySpec(raw, "AES");
        Cipher cipher = Cipher.getInstance("AES");
        cipher.init(Cipher.DECRYPT_MODE, skeySpec);
        byte[] decrypted = cipher.doFinal(encrypted);
        return decrypted;
    }

    public static String toHex(String txt) {
        return toHex(txt.getBytes());
    }
    public static String fromHex(String hex) {
        return new String(toByte(hex));
    }

    public static byte[] toByte(String hexString) {
        int len = hexString.length()/2;
        byte[] result = new byte[len];
        for (int i = 0; i < len; i++)
            result[i] = Integer.valueOf(hexString.substring(2*i, 2*i+2), 16).byte
            Value();
        return result;
    }

    public static String toHex(byte[] buf) {
        if (buf == null)
            return "";
        StringBuffer result = new StringBuffer(2*buf.length);
        for (int i = 0; i < buf.length; i++) {
            appendHex(result, buf[i]);
        }
        return result.toString();
    }
    private final static String HEX = "0123456789ABCDEF";
    private static void appendHex(StringBuffer sb, byte b) {
        sb.append(HEX.charAt((b>>4)&0x0f)).append(HEX.charAt(b&0x0f));
    }
}
```

Asymmetric Keys

All symmetric encryption schemes rely on a single key, which can be very difficult to hide on the phone. If you're hard coding your key in the code, someone will find it and your confidential data will be compromised. Far better to use an asymmetric encryption scheme where there is a public/private key pair, so we can put the public key on the phone and then decrypt it on the server using the hidden private key. There are several libraries out there that we can use, but why not use something

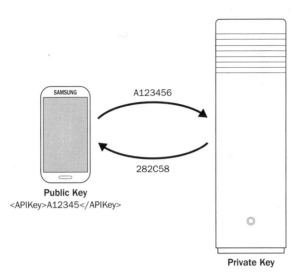

Figure 4-4   Public/private key interchange

provided by Google Security Team, namely Keyczar, which is available from http://keyczar.org.

In this example, we're using Keyczar to create a public/private key to encrypt the API key so that it can be sent to the server to be decrypted. We can use this for passwords or any other confidential information. The difference in this approach is that only the public key is stored on the phone, and we don't really care whether the public key is found because it can't decrypt the data. Only the private key can decrypt the data, and that's sitting on the server.

Figure 4-4 shows a simple example of using Keyczar to create this public/private key interchange. The API key is stored encrypted using the public key in the shared preferences. It doesn't matter whether anyone gains access to the shared preferences given that the data can only be decrypted by the private key. When the app starts, the encrypted API key is sent across the network to the web server where it is decrypted using the private key and the unencrypted key is sent back from the server to the phone where it then does the API calls to Weather Underground.

Listing 4-3 shows the encrypted API key in the res\xml\default_values.xml file.

Listing 4-3 **Encrypted API Key**

```
<PreferenceScreen xmlns:android="http://schemas.android.com/apk/res/android" >
    <EditTextPreference          android:defaultValue="ALu27CGVpdx4yAAAAcnYjT47
EiJ5z-CQar0ivvm0pxdv-b7ACMqxahqvvCRZ7Gvnietk8eDX8mqigFfINVE6ZH11QT8yd2qfjYB5kTtBwy
FqZTvIzNg6y62eApn9C5XO7AtrrRoPo49rHNo23cGtPfVOmPKYfHBQosMP-4C99SVI8uT33AnPqQ9eUQdV2
w8KatLF8qrZELpdElXe-7RYENRVDVn0rb43tJeqbOGp4 _ LWtnQsk _ 0-4xavNFTNnoFJIACF9pKA _ Tmi
oLWxqPvlWPk1tzAHg _ 3N11KaCk98yQfl _ T1o-VrlhQvjhc5Kuymx78HQElhJ068-KPTYKpbVe _ NEWqJr
```

```
Ob9N8nPdB4JDbi6pnfvD _ lIg2kv8n4er5ud6kOEbeIqICQrIjaileLujPh6dv6HHP2 _ MSyVOUMXzAm45c
-0K17G _ 39jLj3vbudt-9EiXleovzxlwo0oqfJylf _ g3PNDFnWYdpISguvYQxhRn9txtuO3odlrTR1WSFL
MAYNTEOQBys8wNNs-hk8OZSzP015lrdX95UuHCeEmjhyuQroAINglFLkh2DjJlstc9lKWyQpsq6bRe _ UF
5qMd9vBaLM _ VaNs7Ps4Y2WEUanEkubTaW5o0TsIjfe8ZrPrdf9Q18enxRlmnLAfvmOk4ZlsQUYOaw403Ya
cq4gMz0nLg8dHU-Fw"
        android:key="EncryptedKey" />
</PreferenceScreen>
```

To generate the key, we first need to create our public and private directory or folder and then create the key pair, as follows.

```
java -jar KeyczarTool.jar create --location=./private --purpose=crypt --name="Key"
--asymmetric=rsa


java -jar KeyczarTool.jar addkey --location=./private --status=primary --size=4096


java -jar KeyczarTool.jar pubkey --location=./private --destination=./public
```

Cut and paste the encrypted API key in the default_values.xml file so it can be referenced in the Android code.

The Android client code is shown in Listing 4-4. We load the encrypted key from the shared preferences on line 41 and send it out to the server.

Listing 4-4 Read API key and send to server

```
package com.riis.restfulwebservice;

import java.io.BufferedReader;
import java.io.InputStreamReader;

import org.apache.http.HttpResponse;
import org.apache.http.client.methods.HttpGet;
import org.apache.http.impl.client.DefaultHttpClient;
import org.apache.http.protocol.BasicHttpContext;
import org.json.JSONObject;

import com.riis.restfulwebservice.R;

import android.os.AsyncTask;
import android.os.Bundle;
import android.preference.PreferenceManager;
import android.app.Activity;
import android.app.ProgressDialog;
import android.content.SharedPreferences;
import android.view.View;
import android.view.View.OnClickListener;
import android.widget.Button;
import android.widget.TextView;

public class RestFulWebservice extends Activity {
```

```
private String endpoint = "http://54.205.41.129:8080/RSAServer/do/decrypt/have
public?text=";

private String protocol;
private String URL1 = "api.wunderground.com/api/";
private String URL2 = "/conditions/q/MI/Troy.json";

private SharedPreferences preferences;
private String encryptedKey;

 @Override
 public void onCreate(Bundle savedInstanceState) {
     super.onCreate(savedInstanceState);
     setContentView(R.layout.restfulwebservice);

     PreferenceManager.setDefaultValues(this, R.xml.default _ values, false);
     // line 41
     preferences = PreferenceManager.getDefaultSharedPreferences(this);
   encryptedKey = preferences.getString("EncryptedKey", null);

     final Button HTTP = (Button) findViewById(R.id.HTTP);
     HTTP.setOnClickListener(new OnClickListener() {
       @Override
       public void onClick(View arg0) {
           try {
             protocol = "http://";
             new WeatherCall().execute(encryptedKey);
           } catch (Exception ex) {
           }
       }
     });

     final Button HTTPS = (Button) findViewById(R.id.HTTPS);
     HTTPS.setOnClickListener(new OnClickListener() {
       @Override
       public void onClick(View arg0) {
           try {
             protocol = "https://";
             new WeatherCall().execute(encryptedKey);
           } catch (Exception ex) {
           }
       }
     });
 }

 private class WeatherCall extends AsyncTask<String, Void, Void> {

     private ProgressDialog dialog = new ProgressDialog(RestFulWebservice.
     this);
     String responseData = "";

     private String fetchData(String URL) {
       try {
           HttpResponse response = (new DefaultHttpClient()).execute(new Http
           Get(URL), (new BasicHttpContext()));
```

```
                StringBuilder builder = new StringBuilder();
                BufferedReader reader = new BufferedReader(new InputStreamReader
                (response.getEntity().getContent()));
                String line;
                while((line = reader.readLine()) != null) {
                    builder.append(line);
                }
                response.getEntity().consumeContent();
                return builder.toString();
        } catch (Exception ex) {
                return ex.getMessage();
        }
    }

    protected void onPreExecute() {
        dialog.setMessage("Please wait..");
        dialog.show();
        ((TextView) findViewById(R.id.output)).setText("");
    }

    protected Void doInBackground(String... params) {
      try {
            responseData = fetchData(protocol + URL1 + new JSONObject(fetchData
          (endpoint + params[0])).getString("result") + URL2);
      } catch (Exception ex) {
      }
      return null;
    }

    protected void onPostExecute(Void unused) {
      try {
            JSONObject observation = new JSONObject(responseData).getJSONObject
            ("current_ observation");
            String result = "";
            result += "Location: " + observation.getJSONObject("display_
            location").getString("full") + "\n";
            result += "Weather: " + observation.getString("weather") + "\n";
            result += "Temperature: " + observation.getString("temperature_
            string");
              ((TextView) findViewById(R.id.output)).setText(result);
      } catch (Exception ex) {
              ((TextView) findViewById(R.id.output)).setText(responseData);
      }
        dialog.dismiss();
    }
  }
}
```

In Listing 4-5, the server receives the API key where it is then decrypted using the private key and returned to the Android client so it can make the call to Weather Underground. The call to the server should be done using HTTPS. All the code can be found on http://github.com/godfreynolan/bulletproof/chapter4.

Listing 4-5   **Keyczar server decrypt**

```
package com.riis.rsaserver;

import javax.ws.rs.*;

import org.json.JSONObject;
import org.keyczar.Crypter;

@Path("/decrypt")
public class RSAServer {
    @Path("havepublic")
    @GET
    @Produces("application/json")
    public String doDecrypt(@QueryParam("text") String text) {
        try {
            return (new JSONObject().put("result", new Crypter(new MyKeyczarReader
            ()).decrypt(text))).toString();
        } catch (Exception ex) {
            return ex.getMessage();
        }
    }
}
```

Ineffective SSL

There are lots of coffee shop attacks where apps like Firesheep (see Figure 4-5) can listen in on the wi-fi for users to enter their usernames and passwords to social media sites. So if you're sending any usernames, passwords, or session tokens, they should always be sent over SSL—you can't assume that no one is listening.

> **Note**
>
> Firesheep only runs on an old version of Firefox 3.x, but there are several sites that provide earlier versions to anyone that wants them, and the Firesheep add-on can still be used.

SSL certs come from a CA, so your users will know that some verification has been done by a third-party agency, confirming that you are who you say you are if they know you're using SSL to communicate to the back-end server. Creating an SSL connection is straightforward in Android, as you can see back in Listing 4-1. However, all is still not 100 percent secure if you're using HTTPS. As we already mentioned, there is no concept of the locked key icon in the browser in Android, so the user is not going to know whether they're sending their information securely or not. Also, it would be great if a mobile app would alert the user if it encountered an invalid cert, similar to the way websites handle it, but there really is no such mechanism in Android. Some apps also make the mistake of accepting SSL certificates issued by anyone, and we'll see how someone can use a tool like Charles Proxy to generate SSL certs on the fly. To further complicate issues, there have been a number of break-ins

Figure 4-5   Firesheep

where bogus CAs were created at Comodo and DigiNotar, so it's not 100 percent rosy on the SSL side. There is some confusion about just how trustworthy SSL really is in Android apps.

One of the best ways to determine whether your application is transmitting data correctly is to use an SSL proxy to perform what is known as a man-in-the-middle attack, which is what we're going to do next.

Man-in-the-Middle Demo

Under the simplest circumstances an Android app operates like a classic client-server app. The client is in on your phone, and the server is a remote back-end server that communicates using RESTful, or sometimes SOAP, web services.

There are times when it's not that simple. You could be playing a game that is mostly taking place on the phone, or the app could be running almost entirely on a remote web server and you're just viewing it through the phone. But normally it works in a client-server fashion.

If your app sends personal information to the remote server, then ideally it should be sending the data over HTTPS, using SSL encryption, to make sure nobody can see the data. But how do you know, or how do your users know, that the information is being transmitted securely given that there's no locked key icon to tell them? The only way to be sure that you're using SSL correctly and that someone can't intercept the information is to try for yourself and perform a man-in-the-middle attack (MITM attack) using a proxy server.

Figure 4-6 shows how we're going to intercept the traffic. Instead of the app talking to the server, the traffic is first intercepted by the proxy server and then passed on to the back-end server. If the traffic isn't encrypted, then the man in the middle can see everything that's transmitted. Even if the traffic is encrypted we can sometimes see the data if the SSL cert has not been installed correctly. If this is the case, we can get around it using our own fake certificate.

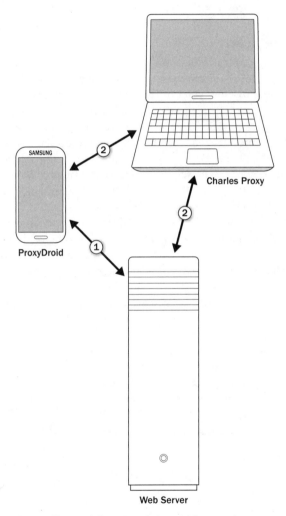

Figure 4-6   Man-in-the-middle attack

Here's what we need to do an MITM attack:

1. Root your phone and install ProxyDroid.
2. Test the traffic with Charles Proxy for HTTP traffic.
3. Self-sign the certificate and retest the SSL traffic.

We're looking to see whether the app ignores SSL errors, or doesn't use SSL at all.

Root Your Phone

For this test we're going to see if the app is securely transmitting data across the network, and we need to do a MITM attack to make sure it's doing what we expect. In this section we're going to show you how to double-check that your app is not going to be open to a MITM attack. We are going to need to root the phone in order to point the network traffic at a proxy. So, once again, we're back to that question we raised in the Preface about white hats and black hats, because to do the test we have no other option than rooting the phone. Rooting the phone means being able to run apps as root or the Unix superuser. We're definitely veering toward black hat territory, and we also run the risk of bricking the phone. We're also showing how to crack an app, but the focus here is on how to protect it rather than how to attack it.

Depending on your phone, it's a pretty straightforward operation to root your phone. If you choose a slightly older Android phone—at time of this writing, a phone running Android 4.1 or 4.2 would be perfect—then you can easily root the phone. Prepaid Android phones from large retail stores or Amazon are usually the best option. New phones running the latest version of Android can usually be rooted, but the chance of them being irreparably damaged are higher because it's typically a multi-stage process. But this isn't so for the earlier versions. Just like the prepaid phone market, the rooting technology is usually a year or so behind the Android releases. So I'm guessing that no matter when you're reading this, the prepaid Android phones are probably going to be the best option if you're looking for a phone to root. And if you turn it into a brick, you haven't wasted a lot of money.

To root your phone you are going to need something that can use a known exploit to gain superuser access. There are different tools for different versions of Android. In this example we're using Cydia Impactor, from www.cydiaimpactor.com (see Figure 4-7).

Figure 4-7   Cydia Impactor

To root the phone, take the following steps with the phone connected via USB to your PC or MAC.

1. Make sure developer options are enabled on the phone.

2. Go to Settings > About phone and tap Build number seven times (if 4.2 or above).

3. Return to the previous screen to find Developer options.

4. Enable USB debugging.

5. Open the Cydia Impactor application.

6. Click on the Start button.

7. Type `adb shell` from the PC command line.

8. Type the `su` command.

If the `su` command is successful and you see a # at the command line, then your phone is rooted.

> **Note**
>
> If you're using a PC, the hardest part when rooting a phone is often getting the correct USB drivers to connect your phone to your PC. This is much less of a problem on the Mac.

Charles Proxy Test

Looking at Figure 4-5 again, we're trying to proxy the traffic via the computer to see if we can intercept the network traffic and make sure it's secure. We need to install ProxyDroid and use that to point the traffic at the computer, and then install Charles Proxy on the computer to see the network traffic.

To conduct a simple MITM attack for unencrypted HTTP and encrypted HTTPS traffic, do the following:

1. From Google Play, install ProxyDroid.

2. Install and open Charles Proxy on your proxy machine.

3. Configure the ProxyDroid host to point at your proxy machine's IP and change the ProxyDroid port to 8888 (the default port on Charles Proxy), as shown in Figure 4-8.

4. Turn on or enable ProxyDroid.

5. Open the Weather Underground app and send both an HTTP and an HTTPS request.

6. Allow a connection attempt to Charles Proxy when asked on your PC or Mac.

Figure 4-8   ProxyDroid

7. View the request and response for the HTTP, which are in cleartext.

8. View the HTTPS traffic; note that 23.193.172.96 is the IP address for api.
   wunderground.com and 443 is the SSL port. Also note that the IP address may
   be different for you.

9. The SSL traffic is encrypted for both the request and the response (see Figure 4-9).

To complete the MITM attack, we need to go one step further. HTTPS works
with server-side or SSL certificates that are provided by a Certificate Authority such as
Verisign or GoDaddy. Users trust that these agencies will validate that the owners of
the website are who they say they are. But, as it turns out, anyone can create their own
SSL cert. We can create a self-signed cert very easily using Charles Proxy, as follows.

1. Click on Proxy -> Proxy Settings.

2. Click on the SSL tab.

3. Make sure Enable SSL proxying is checked.

4. Click on Add and add Host 23.193.172.96 and Port 443 (see Proxy Settings in
   Figure 4-10).

5. Click OK. Charles Proxy is now set up to generate its own certs when it proxies.

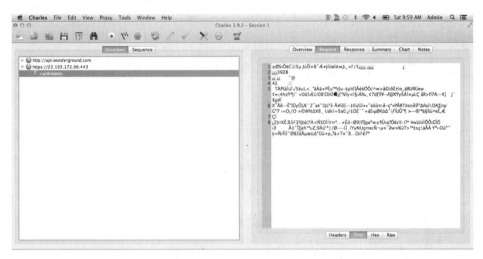

Figure 4-9   Charles Proxy

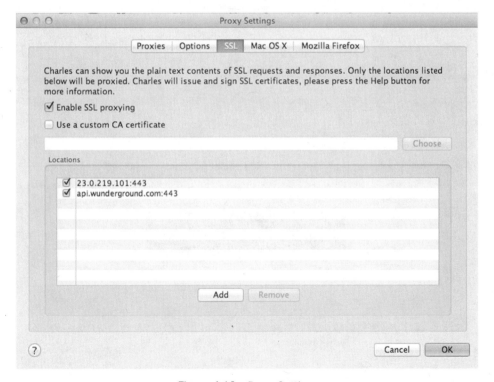

Figure 4-10   Proxy Settings

Now when we try to connect to HTTPS, if our code wasn't handling the certificates correctly we would see the unencrypted traffic. There are several reasons why this might happen—one being that perhaps the developer didn't have a valid SSL cert in development. During that time they bypassed the errors so they could continue to develop the app and then simply forgot to remove the code; or perhaps they're using a valid cert, but not one from the list of Certificate Authorities recognized by Android.

If your code is working correctly you should see a response similar to Figure 4-11. The HTTPS request fails with an error message of "No request was made. Possibly the SSL certificate was rejected."

Our Android app fails gracefully with the error message "No peer certificate" (see Figure 4-12).

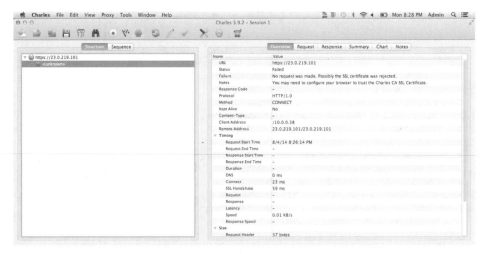

Figure 4-11   HTTPS traffic rejected with self-signed cert

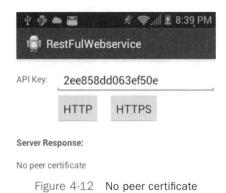

Figure 4-12   No peer certificate

Figure 4-13 shows an example from a well-known jobs website where we're logging in using an employee username and password xriisx03 and password recruiter2. Using the proxy method, we can see that the credentials are clearly visible. If your code is successfully protecting against MITM attacks, you will not see this unencrypted traffic.

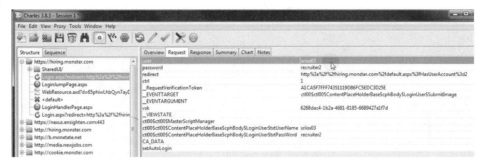

Figure 4-13   Successful MITM attack

Conclusion

In the chapter we looked at how to secure network transmissions and the best approach to storing encryption keys. The primary takeaway here is that if there's any personal information, you're going to need to encrypt the data. What makes the most sense, if at all possible, is to keep all the customer data on the server and not on the phone. If you have to store any data, such as the API key, then asymmetric encryption will keep your data secure. We ended the chapter looking at how to test whether your app will keep your information encrypted during a MITM attack.

Android Databases

In Android development, when we say "databases" we primarily mean SQLite and all of its variants. These are typically small databases used to store or cache user information locally on the device. It would be fair to say that databases and shared preferences contain the bulk of an application's dynamic data that is stored on a phone. In this chapter we're going to look at how developers have used SQLite and, more importantly, how they have tried to secure that data in progressively more secure ways so you don't make the same mistakes.

Android Database Security Issues

Android databases are typically used to cache application data so that it can be retrieved more quickly than doing a web service call to a back-end database server across the Internet. Every app will have its own databases folder. So if the app's package name is com.riis.sqlite3, then you can find all its databases in the /data/data/com.riis.sqlite3 /databases folder. You can see this in Figure 5-1 where we're doing an `adb shell` command to get us a list of the files in the database folder.

Android databases are not a good place to store sensitive information. As we'll see later in the chapter, it is all too easy for someone to do a backup command and quickly find what you're trying to hide.

```
C:\Users\Admin>adb shell ls /data/data/com.riis.sqlite3/databases
tasks.db
tasks.db-journal

C:\Users\Admin>
```

Figure 5-1   SQLite databases on your phone

However, many apps ignore this issue because using SQLite is so convenient for storing data. Facebook keeps a lot of its user information in SQLite databases, which they have openly admitted is for performance reasons. Figure 5-2 shows a Facebook database that's been taken off an Android device using the adb backup command. The "text" column in the threads.db database shows all the thread messages that a user has sent and received in Facebook via the website as well as on the mobile app.

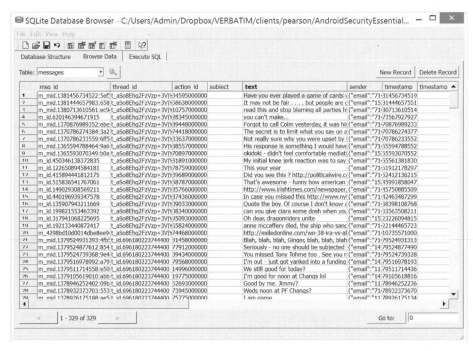

Figure 5-2   Viewing SQLite databases on your PC using SQLitebrowser

SQLite

SQLite is a fully functional database. It has many of the features you would expect in a modern database, such as indexes and stored procedures. You can even do an explain plan for optimizing your queries to find out exactly where your SQL code is spending most of its time.

Any and all of your runtime app information—which includes all the shared preference files and databases—can be backed up by anyone with access to your phone using a USB cable. Because of an oversight at Google, no one running Android after version 4.0 even needs root access—they just need physical access to the phone. To be fair, I think this was an intentional feature, not an oversight. The feature just has significant unintended consequences.

> **Note**
>
> Section §164.312 of the HIPAA standards says the following:
>
> > (a)(1) Standard: Access control. Implement technical policies and procedures for electronic information systems that maintain electronic protected health information to allow access only to those persons or software programs that have been granted access rights as specified in §164.308(a)(4).

Putting any personal health information unencrypted in a SQLite database is not HIPAA compliant because we cannot be sure that only persons that have been granted access have access to the databases. Under most circumstances encrypted information in a SQLite database is also not compliant. A quick way to check whether you have an issue is to put the phone in Airplane mode and then see whether there is any sensitive information, or what is known as Protected Health Information (PHI), being displayed by the application. This will typically tell you that the information is either not encrypted or the encryption key is somewhere on the phone, neither of which is HIPAA compliant.

Backing Up the Database Using `adb`

Let's look at how to write to a SQLite application and how someone can pull the database off the phone. To begin, we need to add a SQLite database to the Android HelloWorld app. Listing 5-1 shows how to add a SQLite database to your Android app.

Listing 5-1   **Adding SQLite to your code**

```
package com.riis.sqlite3;

import java.io.File;
import android.os.Bundle;
import android.app.Activity;
import android.database.sqlite.SQLiteDatabase;              // line 7
public class MainActivity extends Activity {

@Override
protected void onCreate(Bundle savedInstanceState) {
        super.onCreate(savedInstanceState);
        setContentView(R.layout.activity_main);

        InitializeSQLite3();                                 // line 16

    }

    private void InitializeSQLite3() {

        File databaseFile = getDatabasePath("names.db");
        databaseFile.mkdirs();
        databaseFile.delete();
```

```
        SQLiteDatabase database =                              // line 26
            SQLiteDatabase.openOrCreateDatabase(databaseFile, null);

        database.execSQL("create table user(id integer primary key autoincrement,
        " +
                "first text not null, last text not null, " + //    line 28
                "username text not null,  password text not null)");

        database.execSQL("insert into user(first,last,username, password) " +
                "values('Bertie','Ahern','bahern','celia123')");
                // line 31
    }

}
```

To add SQLite to your application, import the library (see line 7), initialize the SQLite database (see line 26), and then create your tables (see line 28) as well as add any initial data (see line 31).

In the example shown we are adding just a single row of data to the database. We are adding a first name, a last name, and a corresponding username and password to our database.

We can now recover the database using the following steps on a compatible phone:

1. Compile the code, push it to your phone or emulator, and make sure it executes.

2. Run the app.

3. Back up the databases using the following command:

   ```
   adb backup com.riis.sqlite3
   ```

4. If all is working, device will respond with "Now unlock your device and confirm the backup operation."

5. On the device or emulator, click Back up my data to enable it to be backed up (see Figure 5-3).

6. The backup file is a tar file with a custom header. We need to download the Android Backup Extractor from https://github.com/nelenkov/android-backup-extractor to get it into a tar format.

7. Convert your backup.ab file using the following command:

   ```
   java -jar abe.jar unpack backup.ab backup.tar
   ```

8. Uncompress your tar file using tar -xvf or 7zip if you're on a Windows machine.

Figure 5-3   Back up my data

9. Change directory to apps/com.riis.sqlite3/db, where you can now find your names.db database.

10. Open names.db in sqlitebrowser from http://sqlitebrowser.org (see Figure 5-4). As you see, the user information is in cleartext.

If you don't have sqlitebrowser, you can always gain access to the sqlite database from the command line (refer ahead to Figure 5-6).

Note that if your backup.ab file is empty, then it's likely that you have used the wrong package name. For commercial apps the best way to find the correct package name is to look at the target ID in the app's Google Play URL (see Figure 5-5 for Facebook's target ID). In this example, to back up the Facebook database you would type the following:

```
adb backup com.facebook.katana
```

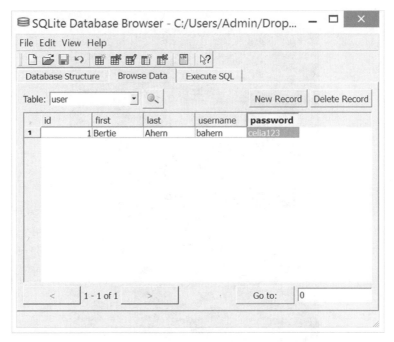

Figure 5-4   View the backup database data using the SQLite browser.

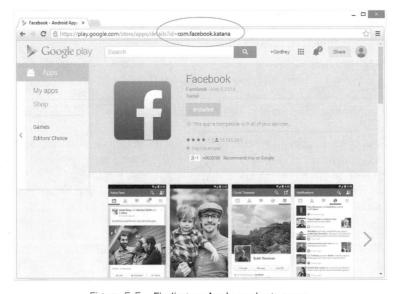

Figure 5-5   Finding an App's package name

to import SQLCipher, add a new `loadLibs` command (line 21) and, as you can see, the `openOrCreateDatabase` now takes a password (line 27).

Listing 5-3   Adding SQLCipher to your SQLite code

```
package com.riis.sqlite3;

import java.io.File;

import android.os.Bundle;
import android.app.Activity;
import net.sqlcipher.database.SQLiteDatabase;                          // line 7

public class MainActivity extends Activity {

    @Override
    protected void onCreate(Bundle savedInstanceState) {
        super.onCreate(savedInstanceState);
        setContentView(R.layout.activity_main);

        InitializeSQLite3();

    }

    private void InitializeSQLite3() {
        SQLiteDatabase.loadLibs(this);                                 // line 21

        File databaseFile = getDatabasePath("names.db");
        databaseFile.mkdirs();
        databaseFile.delete();
        SQLiteDatabase database =                                      // line 27
        SQLiteDatabase.openOrCreateDatabase(databaseFile,"pass123",
        null);

        database.execSQL("create table user(id integer primary key autoincrement,
        " +
                "first text not null, last text not null, " +
                "username text not null, password text not null)");

        database.execSQL("insert into user(first,last,username, password) " +
                "values('Bertie','Ahern','bahern','celia123')");

    }
}
```

Compile and push the app to the phone. Repeat the earlier steps to back up the database onto our computer. You will probably notice that it takes noticeably longer to push the app to the phone, as well as to back it up. This is because of the size of the added libraries.

Again, try to open it in sqlitebrowser or by using the SQLite command line tool. This time the database won't open because it's encrypted with the key pass123.

The best way to open the database is to use the sqlite3 command line tool that comes with SQLCipher. A new step is required whereby we need to tell the database what the key is before it will allow us to do any SQL queries on the tables.

```
sqlite> PRAGMA key='pass123';
```

Figure 5-7 shows how to view the database using the new password.

You may also encounter databases that were created with earlier versions of the SQLCipher libraries. These can be opened using the following PRAGMA command after the PRAGMA key command.

```
sqlite> PRAGMA key='pass123';
sqlite> PRAGMA kdf_iter = 4000;
```

This tells the sqlite tool that the key definition file has a lower iteration count than the current version.

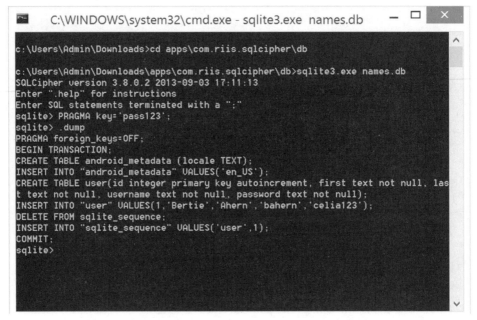

Figure 5-7   Viewing an encrypted database from command line SQLite

Finding the Key

Now that SQLCipher has encrypted the database, our security problem shifts to "Where can we hide the key?" If we can find the key, then we're going to be able to open the database, just like we did in Chapter 2. We can take the following steps to pull the APK off the device.

1. The APK is in the /data/app folder on the phone. It will also be called the same package name we used in the `adb backup` command but with -1.apk appended. The complete command to get the APK off the phone is the following:

   ```
   adb pull /data/app/com.riis.sqlcipher-1.apk
   ```

2. Convert the APK back into a jar file using the `dex2jar` command:

   ```
   dex2jar com.riis.sqlcipher-1.apk
   ```

3. We can now view the source using a Java decompiler, in this case JD-GUI. Figure 5-8 shows the code for the MainActivity.java file and clearly shows that the password is pass123.

In the next section we'll look at our options for hiding the key.

Figure 5-8   Viewing the SQLCipher key using JD-GUI

Hiding the Key

One of the most fundamental decisions that you're going to face as a mobile developer is what encryption to use to hide sensitive information and whether you're going to leave the information on the phone or not.

In this section we're going to look at a number of different ways that other developers have tried to solve this problem. These examples come from real-world Android apps that we've audited over the years. They each get progressively better at hiding an encryption key for the database itself or for fields in the database, such as the password.

Security on Android is almost always a battle between security and ease of use. App developers want to make it easy for people to use, and they don't think it's a good idea to make someone log into the phone multiple times.

And while many of these examples look like very naive implementations, we have the benefit of hindsight and can probably assume that the developers were not aware that someone could gain access to their code and encryption keys so easily. If you're using some sort of symmetrical key encryption where the encrypted data, as well as the encrypted key, are on the phone, then you're leaving yourself open to attack.

Ask Each Time

Possibly the safest way to encrypt your database is to ask for the key each time, either using a PIN code or a password. The first time the user opens the app they're asked for the key, which is then used to encrypt the database.

If the user wants to access any data on the app, then the next time they use the app they have to remember their key and reenter it. The key is stored in the user's head and not on your phone.

The downside of this is that the user has to log in to the phone each time they open your app. And depending on the key size it may also be open to a brute-force attack. Certainly a four-digit pin code is not very secure.

Listing 5-4 shows an example of how to use a login password to encrypt the database. The password is captured as the user is logging in on line 31; it's then passed to `initializeSQLCipher` as a string on line 35 and used as the SQLCipher key when we open the database on line 45.

Listing 5-4   **Using a Login password to encrypt the database**

```
public class LoginActivity extends Activity {

    private Button loginButton;

    @Override
    protected void onCreate(Bundle savedInstanceState) {
```

```java
        super.onCreate(savedInstanceState);
        setContentView(R.layout.login_screen);
        initializeViews();
        bindListenersToViews();

    }

    private void initializeViews() {
        loginButton = (Button) findViewById(R.id.login_button);

    }

    private void bindListenersToViews() {
        loginButton.setOnClickListener(new View.OnClickListener() {
            @Override
            public void onClick(View v) {
                    loginToApp();
            }
    });
    }

    private void loginToApp() {
        EditText usernameField = (EditText) findViewById(R.id.username_field);
        EditText passwordField =           // line 31
(EditText) findViewById(R.id.password_field);
        EditText emailField = (EditText) findViewById(R.id.email_field);


        InitializeSQLCipher(passwordField.getText().toString());          // line 35

    }

    private void InitializeSQLCipher(String pwd) {
        SQLiteDatabase.loadLibs(this);
        File databaseFile = getDatabasePath("names.db");
        databaseFile.mkdirs();
        databaseFile.delete();

        SQLiteDatabase database =                                 // line 45
SQLiteDatabase.openOrCreateDatabase(databaseFile, pwd, null);

        database.execSQL("create table user(id integer primary key autoincrement,
        " +
                    "first text not null, last text not null, " +
                    "username text not null,  password text not null)");

        database.execSQL("insert into user(first,last,username, password) " +
                    "values('Bertie','Ahern','bahern','celia123')");
    }
}
```

Shared Preferences

The next implementation is to hide the key in the shared preferences and then load it each time the app is opened. There are two variations on this theme. A typical app will ask the user to encrypt the app the first time and save the key in the shared preferences. Listing 5-5 shows how to write and load our encryption key from a shared preferences file.

Listing 5-5   **Storing passwords in the shared preferences file**

```
private void saveLastSuccessfulCreds() {
    String username =
((EditText) findViewById(R.id.username_field)).getText().toString();
    String password =                                              // line 3
((EditText) findViewById(R.id.password_field)).getText().toString();

    SharedPreferences.Editor editor = sharedPrefs.edit();
    editor.putString(SettingsActivity.LAST_USERNAME_KEY, username);
    editor.putString(SettingsActivity.LAST_PASSWORD_KEY, password);   // line 7
    editor.commit();
}

private void loadLastSuccessfulCreds() {
    String lastUsername =
sharedPrefs.getString(SettingsActivity.LAST_USERNAME_KEY, "");
    String lastPassword =                                          // line 13
sharedPrefs.getString(SettingsActivity.LAST_PASSWORD_KEY, "");

    ((EditText) findViewById(R.id.username_field)).setText(lastUsername);
    ((EditText) findViewById(R.id.password_field)).setText(lastPassword); //line 16
}
```

The adb backup command will not only recover the databases, it will also recover the shared preferences files. Figure 5-9 shows a screenshot of someone viewing a shared preferences file on the phone itself.

Alternatively, the app can load an app-specific username and password when the app is first opened. Android will load data from the resources/xml folder and store it in shared preferences. Listing 5-6 shows how to load the key from the resources folder.

Listing 5-6   **Loading the SQLCipher key from the resources folder**

```
<PreferenceScreen xmlns:android="http://schemas.android.com/apk/res/android" >

<EditTextPreference
    android:defaultValue="pass1234"
    android:key="myKey" />

</PreferenceScreen>
```

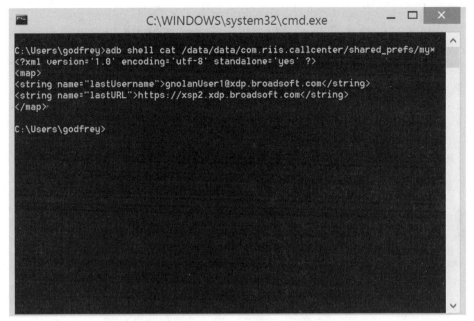

Figure 5-9   Viewing shared preferences files

The advantage of this is that it's very easy to use; it encrypts the database without any user input. The disadvantage is that it's very easy for someone to find the key and decrypt the phones. For example, the apktool—available from https://code.google.com/p/android-apktool/—will convert an APK's resources back into xml using the following command:

```
java -jar apktool.jar d com.riis.sqlcipher-1.apk
```

In the Code

We can see from the SQLCipher code example earlier in Figure 5-8 that we can't simply hard code our key in the SQLCipher class because someone is going to find it when they decompile your APK. If we create a security scale showing level of difficulty—from 1 to 10, where 1 is your kid brother and 10 is a foreign government—then we're close to 1 or 2 in the level of difficulty to reverse engineer an APK to decompile the code.

A couple of years ago, using a single security key for everyone's app was common practice in Android development. More recently, developers have moved to generating the key and making it device-specific using the device's attributes, such as device_id, android_id, and any number of phone-specific attributes such as BUILD ID's, and Build.MODEL and Build.MANUFACTURER. This is then concatenated together and is a unique key for that phone or tablet. Listing 5-7 shows how you might do that. It takes the device's unique Android ID and the Device ID (assuming it's not a tablet) as well as a whole array of phone information. All of this information is concatenated together and converted into an md5 digest or hash value.

So far, so good. It protects the app from any potential targeted malware that would use a decompiled key to attack the app on lots of different phones. However, although the key isn't the same on every device, the algorithm is the same. And it's a small step if the code can be decompiled to figure out how to recreate the recipe for generating the key, so ultimately it's only slightly more secure than using the same key.

Listing 5-7 **Device-specific keys**

```
android_id =
    Secure.getString(getBaseContext().getContentResolver(),Secure.ANDROID_ID);
tManager = (TelephonyManager) this.getSystemService(Context.TELEPHONY_SERVICE);
device_id = tManager.getDeviceId();


String str1 = Build.BOARD + Build.BRAND + Build.CPU_ABI + Build.DEVICE +
    Build.DISPLAY + Build.FINGERPRINT + Build.HOST + Build.ID + Build.MANUFACTURER
+
    Build.MODEL + Build.PRODUCT + Build.TAGS + Build.TYPE + Build.USER;
String key2 = md5(str1 + device_id + android_id);
```

In the NDK

If the Java code in Android can be reverse engineered so easily, then it makes sense to write it in some other language that isn't so easily decompiled. Some developers hide their keys in C++ using the Native Developer Kit (NDK). The NDK enables developers to write code as a C++ library. This can be useful if you want to try to hide any keys in binary code. And, unlike Java code, C++ cannot be decompiled, only disassembled.

Listing 5-8 shows some simple C++ code for returning the "pass123" key to encrypt the database.

Listing 5-8 **Hiding the key in the NDK**

```
#include <string.h>
#include <jni.h>

jstring Java_com_riis_sqlndk_MainActivity_invokeNativeFunction(JNIEnv* env,
jobject javaThis) {
  return (*env)->NewStringUTF(env, "pass123");
}
```

Listing 5-9 shows the Android code to call the NDK method correctly. Line 11 does the JNI library call, the function is defined on line 14, and then we call the function that returns the key on line 21. The `sqlndk.c` file needs to be in a `jni` folder. And because it's C++ code, we're going to need a make file.

Listing 5-9   **Calling the NDK code from Android**

```
import java.io.File;

import net.sqlcipher.database.SQLiteDatabase;
import android.os.Bundle;
import android.app.Activity;
import android.app.AlertDialog;

public class MainActivity extends Activity {

    static {
        System.loadLibrary("sqlndk");                          // line 11
        }

    private native String invokeNativeFunction();              // line 14

    @Override
    protected void onCreate(Bundle savedInstanceState) {
        super.onCreate(savedInstanceState);
        setContentView(R.layout.activity_main);

        String sqlkey = invokeNativeFunction();                // line 21
        new AlertDialog.Builder(this).setMessage(sqlkey).show();

        InitializeSQLCipher(sqlkey);


    }

    private void InitializeSQLCipher(String initKey) {
        SQLiteDatabase.loadLibs(this);
        File databaseFile = getDatabasePath("tasks.db");
        databaseFile.mkdirs();
        databaseFile.delete();
        SQLiteDatabase database =
            SQLiteDatabase.openOrCreateDatabase(databaseFile, initKey, null);
        database.execSQL("create table tasks" +
                " (id integer primary key autoincrement,title text not null)");
        database.execSQL("insert into tasks(title) values('Placeholder 1')");
    }
}
```

Listing 5-10 shows the corresponding Android.mk file. The C++ code is compiled using the `ndk-build` command that comes with the Android NDK tools. `ndk-build` is run from a `cgywin` command line if you're on Windows.

Listing 5-10   **NDK makefile**

```
LOCAL_PATH := $(call my-dir)

include $(CLEAR _ VARS)

# Here we give our module name and source file(s)
LOCAL _ MODULE      := sqlndk
LOCAL _ SRC _ FILES := sqlndk.c

include $(BUILD _ SHARED _ LIBRARY)
```

But we're not there yet. Even though we can no longer decompile the code, we can disassemble it. Looking at Figure 5-10 you can see where the library, opened up in a hexadecimal editor, shows the key very clearly at the end of the hexidecimal strings in the file.

If you're going to use the NDK, then choose hexadecimal-like text so that it doesn't stand out in a hex editor. We can also take the earlier approach and use some device-specific or app-specific characteristic and generate a unique app key in NDK just like we can in native Android code. Listing 5-11 shows how you can use the app

Figure 5-10   Viewing the NDK password

ID as a unique key, which will be different every time the app is installed on a different phone. It uses a function called `getlogin()` to find out the login ID, which in this case is the `app_id`.

Listing 5-11   **Using the App ID for the database key**

```
#include <string.h>
#include <jni.h>
#include <unistd.h>

jstring Java_com_riis_sqlndk_MainActivity_invokeNativeFunction(JNIEnv* env,
jobject javaThis) {

    return (*env)->NewStringUTF(env, (char *)getlogin());

}
```

However, neither of these approaches is ultimately enough to stop someone from reading the binary. But it is a better option to consider if you have no other choice than to put the API or encryption keys on the device. Disassembled code rapidly becomes more difficult to understand as it gets further away from these simple hello-world examples.

Web Services

The safest option for any type of device is to store the key, or the algorithm for generating your key, remotely and to access it via secure web services. This has already been covered in previous chapters. The disadvantage to this is that the Android device will need to be connected to the Internet when you open the database, which might not be acceptable to the end user.

But the message should be clear by now that any keys stored on the phone are open to being hacked in ways similar to what we've shown in this section. We'll go into more detail in the next chapter about what to do to protect your web server and your web server traffic from prying eyes.

SQL Injection

SQL injection refers to when the attacker taints the data with a SQL statement. We said earlier that SQLite is a fully functional database, so, just like your SQL Server or MySQL box, it is just as susceptible to SQL injection if you are not careful. SQL injection typically works by adding data to the querystring or adding data in a form field to give the hacker access to the database or unauthorized logins. And while SQL injection is usually something used for attacking a web view or a web service, it can also be an attack on an Activity. Figure 5-11 shows a simple SQL injection example.

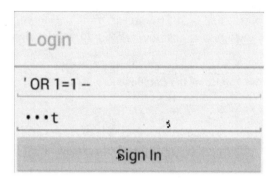

Figure 5-11   Classic SQL injection attack

If we look at the `checkLogin` code in Listing 5-12 we can see that the SQL query is passed directly to the database. So if we log in with a username of `' OR 1=1 --'` and password of `test`, the query to SQLite will be the following string:

```
select * from login where USERNAME = '' OR 1=1 --' and PASSWORD = 'test'
```

Listing 5-12   **Login unprotected from SQL injection**

```
public boolean checkLogin(String param1, String param2)
{
    boolean bool = false;

    Cursor cursor = db.rawQuery("select * from login where USERNAME = '" +
    // line 5
        param1 + "' and PASSWORD = '" + param2 + "';", null);

    if (cursor != null) {
        if (cursor.moveToFirst())
            bool = true;
        cursor.close();
    }
    return bool;
}
```

Because of the `OR 1=1` portion of the string and the `--`, which comments out the rest of the SQL query, this will always be a true condition. The result is that the user can log in without needing a real username and password.

To fix this we need to sanitize any user-entered data and assume it can't be trusted. We can do this either by using regular expressions to check that it's what we're expecting—for example, a valid email address—or by using SQL prepared statements. Or better still, we can do both.

To fix our `checkLogin` code we're going to change the SQL to use prepared statements. Listing 5-13 shows a modified `checkLogin`, which now uses prepared statements on line 5. Here the injected SQL becomes a parameter and can no longer cut off the SQL statement.

Listing 5-13 **Protecting code using prepared statements**

```
public boolean checkSecureLogin(String param1, String param2)
{
    boolean bool = false;

    Cursor cursor = db.rawQuery("select * from login where " +      // line 5
        "USERNAME = ? and PASSWORD = ?", new String[]{param1, param2});

    if (cursor != null) {
        if (cursor.moveToFirst())
            bool = true;
        cursor.close();
    }
    return bool;
}
```

Conclusion

In this chapter we've looked at options to make your databases more secure. If you're going to store customer information, we've covered how to use SQLCipher to encrypt the data as well as the various schemes developers have used to hide the key and keep the data safely encrypted.

The only 100 percent secure way to hide any encryption key is to keep it off the phone, and even then you must make sure it's transmitted securely and not cached anywhere. Every other alternative that we looked at had limitations, some more obvious than others. None of these alternatives would be HIPAA compliant. Ask yourself the question, "Would the security of my app be compromised if someone could read my code?" If the answer is yes, then the app is not HIPAA compliant.

Web Server Attacks

It might seem odd that a book on Android development has a chapter on web server attacks. The majority of the Android apps that we've audited have a significant server component.

The mantra in this book so far has been: Do not put anything of value on the client. But this is all in vain if the server is not secure. You need to make sure that the back door, as well as the front door, is secure.

Hacking into a mobile app, a website, or an ATM usually involves finding something that should be locked down but for some reason isn't. For example, in the last chapter we talked about an app that had encrypted passwords in the shared preferences but left the same password unencrypted in the SQLite database. So even if the encryption key is found in the code, there really isn't much point in decrypting the password if it's already available elsewhere. Similarly, if you're not securing your web services, then you're leaving yourself open to attack.

We're also going to talk about Hybrid apps, which typically use online web pages to display information within your Android app. Web pages within a mobile app can be a very effective way to secure financial applications, for example, so they shouldn't be completely discounted as part of your toolkit. But if you're not careful you can also introduce new security holes in your application. In this chapter we look at some of those pitfalls that you want to avoid.

Web Services

In the last chapter we talked about how to keep web service API keys hidden, whether that's using SSL or by using some sort of asymmetric encryption, for example, public/private keys. It is still very common to send API keys in the query string or as clear-text. But if your app is sending API keys via HTTP or you're using some sort of symmetric encryption key that's hard coded in your Android app, then it's probably going to be found if someone goes looking. And updating API keys because your old one has been compromised can be a very painful process, for both you and your users. In

Chapter 3 we also touched on using hacked usernames and passwords from other websites to test whether your users are reusing the same usernames and passwords on your site.

In this section we're going to expand what we need to do to protect your web services on the server as opposed to on the client. Most mobile apps that do real work will in some way connect to a back-end web server. If the communication is via a web service, then this either can be via SOAP or the more commonly used RESTful Web Service.

The best thing about RESTful Web Services from a programmer's point of view is that RESTful APIs are consistent across platforms and web servers. The URL or URI will be something like http://riis.com/resources for all items or http://riis.com /resources/item17 for a specific item, and you can typically perform GET, POST, PUT, and DELETE actions on the item or collections of items. This consistency makes it easy to attempt a hack, especially with testing tools such as SoapUI (see Figure 6-1) that allow us to automate the process. SoapUI is available from http://soapui.org.

SOAP services typically have a publicly available Web Service Description Language (WSDL) that defines in detail all the available calls or methods and their parameters. The WSDL can be accessed often by adding ?wsdl to the web service, for example, https://riisllc.sugarondemand.com/soap.php?wsdl.

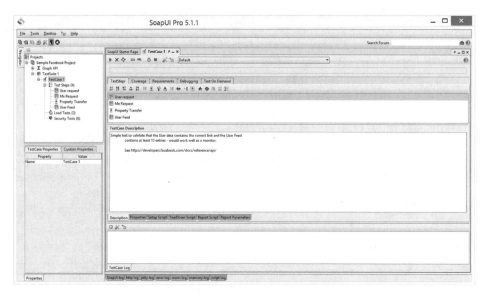

Figure 6-1   SoapUI

OWASP Web Services Cheat Sheet

Although there isn't an OWASP Web Services Top 10, there is an OWASP Web Service Security Cheat Sheet that can help you come to grips with where to start in securing your web services. We've looked at OWASP in previous chapters and, again, it stands for Open Web Application Security Project. It is one of the main industry standards for secure coding practices.

The OWASP standards are described in the following sections.

1. Transport Confidentiality

All communication should be using SSL to prevent man-in-the-middle attacks.

2. Server Authentication

Android apps should not ignore any SSL cert errors. The web server should use an SSL cert from a recognized Certificate Authority (CA).

3. User Authentication

Do not assume that client login using cached data is good enough; the user should also be authenticated against the server's database. OWASP also recommends using SSL client certs. These are certs used to identify the user as opposed to the server; see www.symantec.com/connect/blogs/client-certificates-vs-server-certificates-what -s-difference. This would be very unusual in the mobile world.

4. Message Integrity

The public key is readily available, so it doesn't give you message integrity. But if you sign the message sent from the server to the client with the private key, this can be validated using the public key.

5. Message Confidentiality

SSL does not guarantee that a received message is still secure. Use strong encryption for any messages that are kept for later use as they are received so they can't be decrypted.

6. Authorization

Make sure any web service access is authorized. Authorized access to http://riis.com /users should not also give access to http://riis.com/admin_users. Better still, move any admin access to a different server.

7. Schema Validation

Validate your soap messages against their well-defined XSD. Use an industry-standard parser, and not regex, to ensure there are no gaps in your validation.

8. Content Validation

Validate messages before consuming to protect against XML bombs. An XML bomb is an XML string that takes advantage of XML parsers. A single XML file when parsed rapidly consumes the server memory and crashes the server (see the Billion Laughs examples at http://en.wikipedia.org/wiki/Billion_laughs).

9. Output Encoding

Outbound web service responses should be stripped of any scripts to limit the chance of XSS (Cross-Site Scripting).

10. Virus Protection

Attachments are valid in SOAP and REST. Use a virus scanner on any attachments or any large base64 encoded strings.

11. Message Size

Keep SOAP and REST message responses small to limit denial-of-service attacks.

12. Availability

To date there have been some significant articles in the press about web service attacks for mobile devices, such as Snapchat (www.forbes.com/sites/timworstall/2013/12/26 /snapchats-api-is-hacked-and-exploits-allowing-phone-number-collection-and-bogus -account-creation-published/) and Twitter (http://techcrunch.com/2013/02/01 /twitter-sends-out-emails-to-250k-users-who-may-have-been-compromised-says -hack-was-not-related-to-yesterdays-outage/).

Both hacks require the web server to allow the hackers to send thousands, if not hundreds of thousands, of web service requests to gain username and password information. Likewise, many of these brute-force web service attacks would be nowhere near as effective if the web server recognized patterns of activity. At the very least it should block access from IP addresses that send rapid-fire login requests. Decide on how many requests or type of requests you will accept for a single IP (for example, ten per second or per minute) and deny access until the next time period. If the requests persist, add them to a blacklist (see http://en.wikipedia.org/wiki/Iproute2 for information on using iproute2 tools or use the command `ip ro add blackhole IP.ADDRESS. TO.BLACKLIST`).

There are also many IP blacklists—such as ThreatLog at http://api.threatlog.com/ or Spamhaus at www.spamhaus.org/—that are good places to start, rather than having to create a IP blacklist from scratch.

Replay Attacks

While we successfully hid the API key in the last chapter by encrypting it on the server, there is nothing to stop someone else from sending the same encrypted password from a different app to defeat your efforts. You can stop these replay attacks by encrypting your API key together with a one-time only randomly generated number or GUID, known as a nonce. The nonce and API key are sent to the server for API authentication, and the API key and a new nonce are sent back to the client to be saved in the shared preferences after each login for the next use. Every generated nonce is saved when created and marked as used once it has been sent from any client. If you're using PHP on your web server, then the PHP Nonce Library is a good place to start (see http://fullthrottledevelopment.com/php-nonce-library, or if you're using Java see https://code.google.com/p/openid4java/source/browse/trunk/src/org/openid4java/consumer/InMemoryNonceVerifier.java, for some sample code to verify against replay attacks).

Cross Platform

Cross-platform apps are normally written using some third-party technology, such as PhoneGap or Appcelerator Titanium, which allows the same HTML to be wrapped in an iOS or Android skin. The code can be compiled to target iOS or Android. The attraction of these cross-platform tools is that only one codebase is needed for multiple platforms. PhoneGap is written in HTML5 and JavaScript, and the code can be seen by simply unzipping the APK (see Figure 6-2).

We can see how the app is laid out. If we decompile the much-smaller-than-usual classes.dex file (see Figure 6-3) and look at the code, it's obvious that the code is a harness that loads the HTML and JavaScript, which is in the assets/www folder. It also acts as a bridge to some of the device's functionality, such as the camera, audio, and even the contact list.

Going back to the assets/www folder, we can see that the app is written in HTML5 and JavaScript. As with classic Android apps everything is viewable, but we also can see the comments, so you need to be extra careful what you put in production (see lines 3 and 4 in Listing 6-1).

Listing 6-1   **Comments in cross-platform code**

```
//
//
// Temp Hack to get working          (line 3)
// until Baz can pass the full account number in webservice (line 4)
//
//
// get the full account number and store for modify and earliest
payment date
for (var i = 0; i < Accounts.length; i++)
```

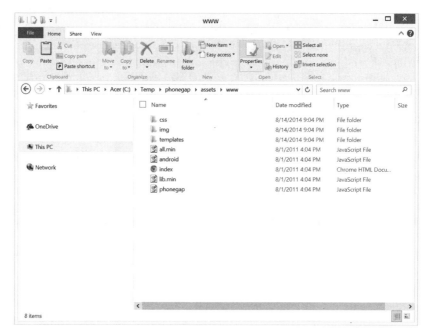

Figure 6-2   Unzipped cross-platform APK

Figure 6-3   Decompiled cross-platform code

```
{
            var account = Accounts[i];
            //Log("Selected Accts: "+account.AccountNumber+'
            '+account.AccountName+' '+SelectedPayment.AccountName+'
            '+SelectedPayment.AccountNumber);
            if (account.AccountName == pendingPaymentInstance.From
            AccountName)
            {
                //Log("account.AccountNumber="+account.AccountNumber);
                pendingPaymentInstance.FromAccountNumberFull =
                account.AccountNumber;
                break;
            }
        }
```

If you are going to write a cross-platform app using PhoneGap, then consider using one of the many JavaScript compressors on the Web to remove the comments and make the JavaScript a bit harder to read. Here are some examples:

- http://www.crockford.com/javascript/jsmin.html
- http://jscompress.com/
- http://dean.edwards.name/packer/
- http://yui.github.io/yuicompressor/

Listing 6-2 shows the code before obfuscation.

Listing 6-2   Code before obfuscation

```
window.$ = $telerik.$;
$(document).ready(function() {
movePageElements();

var text = $('textarea').val();

if (text != "")
$('textarea').attr("style", "display: block;");
else
$('textarea').attr("style", "display: none;");

//cleanup
text = null;
});

function movePageElements() {
var num = null;
var pagenum = $(".pagecontrolscontainer");
if (pagenum.length > 0) {
var num = pagenum.attr("pagenumber");
if ((num > 5) && (num < 28)) {
var x = $('div#commentbutton');
```

```
$("div.buttonContainer").prepend(x);
}
else {
$('div#commentbutton').attr("style", "display: none;");
}
}

//Add in dropshadowing
if ((num > 5) && (num < 28)) {
var top = $('.dropshadow-top');
var middle = $('#dropshadow');
var bottom = $('.dropshadow-bottom');
$('#page').prepend(top);
$('#topcontainer').after(middle);
middle.append($('#topcontainer'));
middle.after(bottom);
}

//cleanup
num = null;
pagenum = null;
top = null;
middle = null;
bottom=null;
}

function expandCollapseDiv(id) {
$telerik.$(id).slideToggle("slow");
}

function expandCollapseHelp() {
$('.helpitems').slideToggle("slow");

//Add in dropshadowing
if ($('#helpcontainer').length) {
$('#help-dropshadow-bot').insertAfter('#helpcontainer');
$('#help-dropshadow-bot').removeAttr("style");
}
}

function expandCollapseComments() {
var style = $('textarea').attr("style");
if (style == "display: none;")
$('textarea').fadeIn().focus();
else
$('textarea').fadeOut();

//cleanup
style = null;
}
```

Listing 6-3 shows the same code after it has been obfuscated by JSCompress, from http://jscompress.com. Obviously, it's a lot harder to read and the comments are gone.

Listing 6-3   **Code after obfuscation**

```
window.$=$telerik.$;$(document).ready(function(){movePageElements();var a=$
("textarea").val();if(a!=""){$("textarea").attr("style","display: block;")}
else{$("textarea").attr("style","display: none;")}a=null});function movePage
Elements(){var e=null;var b=$(".pagecontrolscontainer");if(b.length>0){var e=b
.attr("pagenumber");if((e>5)&&(e<28)){var a=$("div#commentbutton");$("div.button
Container").prepend(a)}else{$("div#commentbutton").attr("style","display: none;
")}}if((e>5)&&(e<28)){var f=$(".dropshadow-top");var d=$("#dropshadow");var c=$
(".dropshadow-bottom");$("#page").prepend(f);$("#topcontainer").after(d);d.append
($("#topcontainer"));d.after(c)}e=null;b=null;f=null;d=null;c=null}function
expandCollapseDiv(a){$telerik.$(a).slideToggle("slow")}function expandCollapse
Help(){$(".helpitems").slideToggle("slow");if($("#helpcontainer").length){$("#
help-dropshadow-bot").insertAfter("#helpcontainer");$("#help-dropshadow-bot")
.removeAttr("style")}}function expandCollapseComments(){var a=$("textarea").attr
("style");if(a=="display: none;"){$("textarea").fadeIn().focus()}else{$("textarea")
.fadeOut()}a=null};
```

But be warned: Although these compressors will remove comments and can even base64 encode your files, they can all be returned to fairly readable JavaScript using a JavaScript formatter such as http://jsbeautifier.org/.

A good alternative is to use Closure (https://developers.google.com/closure /compiler/), which will compile your JavaScript into better JavaScript. It won't make the JavaScript unreadable, but it will make it more obscure than the original code.

To run Closure on your files, go to the online Closure Compiler, http:// closure-compiler.appspot.com/home, and choose the advanced option (see Figure 6-4). Or you can run it from the command line as follows:

```
java -jar compiler.jar --js _ output _ file=out.js in1.js in2.js in3.js ...
```

Similar to our discussion about obfuscating in Chapter 2, test the new JavaScript code using Calabash or some other Cucumber tool to make sure you haven't changed your code's functionality.

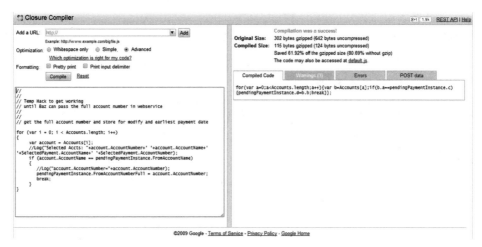

Figure 6-4   Online Closure Compiler

WebView Attacks

Hybrid apps, as opposed to cross-platform apps, don't use any third-party applications such as PhoneGap or Titanium; they are simply web pages within an Android app (see Listing 6-4, which loads the Google home web page into an Android app).

Listing 6-4   **WebView**

```
public class WebViewActivity extends Activity {

  private WebView webView;

  public void onCreate(Bundle savedInstanceState) {
    super.onCreate(savedInstanceState);
    setContentView(R.layout.webview);

    webView = (WebView) findViewById(R.id.webView1);
    webView.getSettings().setJavaScriptEnabled(true);
    webView.loadUrl("http://www.google.com");

  }

}
```

WebView can be very useful from a security perspective because you can put your credit card payments' functionality on a more secure web server. The user still enters their credit card information in your app, but by entering it into a web browser without having to leave the mobile app (see Figure 6-5).

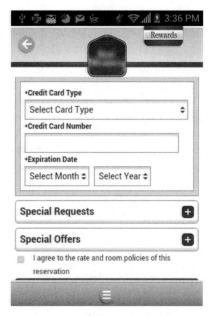

Figure 6-5   Best Western credit card payment using WebView

But be careful what information you cache or what information your tool is saving. Be sure to back up your data and double-check the /app/<app name>/db folder. Open the webview.db using sqlite3 or SQLiteBrowser and make sure that you're not caching credit card or other personal information. See Listing 6-5 for an example of what this would look like.

Listing 6-5   **Data dump of webview.db with credit card information**

```
CREATE TABLE formdata ( _ id INTEGER PRIMARY KEY, urlid INTEGER, name TEXT, value
TEXT, UNIQUE (urlid, name, value) ON CONFLICT IGNORE);
INSERT INTO formdata VALUES(1,3,'firstName','godfrey');
INSERT INTO formdata VALUES(2,4,'firstName','godfrey');
INSERT INTO formdata VALUES(3,4,'address1','12744 main st');
INSERT INTO formdata VALUES(4,4,'lastName','nolan');
INSERT INTO formdata VALUES(5,4,'city','Royal Oak');
INSERT INTO formdata VALUES(6,4,'postalCode','48067');
INSERT INTO formdata VALUES(7,4,'email','godfrey@riis.com');
INSERT INTO formdata VALUES(8,4,'confirmEmail','godfrey@riis.com');
INSERT INTO formdata VALUES(9,4,'telephone','2485559999');
INSERT INTO formdata VALUES(10,3,'address1','12744 main st');
INSERT INTO formdata VALUES(11,3,'lastName','Nolan');
INSERT INTO formdata VALUES(12,3,'city','Royal Oak');
INSERT INTO formdata VALUES(13,4,'lastName','Nolan');
INSERT INTO formdata VALUES(14,4,'creditCardNumber',41111111111111111111);
INSERT INTO formdata VALUES(15,6,'emailAddress','godfrey@riis.com');
```

> **Note**
>
> You can also create your own web page using WebViews. The following code creates a Hello World HTML page.
>
> ```
> String customHtml = "<html><body><h1>Hello, Google</h1></body></html>";
> webView.loadData(customHtml, "text/html", "UTF-8");
> ```

If you are using WebViews, then you also need to be aware of the dangers of cross-site scripting (XSS) as well as SQL injection.

SQL injection is when the attacker adds extra SQL in the query string or adds data in a form field, which gives them access to more data than they should have or, alternatively, bypasses your authentication. The classic example is to add the string ' or '1'=1 to an unprotected form to always return true.

Use SQL prepared statements to protect against SQL injection and avoid concatenating strings together to form your SQL query.

Cross-site scripting is when a malicious script is entered into a web page to produce an undesired effect. To protect against XSS, the input data needs to be parsed to ensure it's not a script using regular expressions. Or, better still, just set I to false as follows:

```
webView.getSettings().setJavaScriptEnabled(false);
```

SQL Injection

In the last chapter we looked at how to use SQL injection to log in to an app without a username and password. SQL injection can also mean hacking query strings or REST APIs to see if you can find other account data. In Figure 6-6 we're using a tool called Burp Suite, which is very similar to the Charles Proxy tool we've used for man-in-the-middle attacks. It's available from http://portswigger.net//.

As the figure shows, we can call the web service directly and the account balance for both the checking and savings accounts is $0.00 for account number 1234567899.

Figure 6-6   Viewing the account information from Burp Suite

But what if we change the account to 1234567890 and do the call again? In Figure 6-7 we see that the checking account for the hacked account is $947.30. Web services need to be locked down so that they don't allow someone to read information from someone else's account. Nobody should be able to access the account number directly; it should be a combination of terms that cannot be guessed that map to the account number.

Figure 6-7   We can see the checking account balance.

XSS

Android apps, as we've seen, can be native, HTML5, or a hybrid app with some HTML but mostly native Java code. If you are using a WebView app, then it's important to think carefully about setting the `setJavaScriptEnabled` to true in your WebViews.

Listing 6-6 is a quick demo that shows a WebView with an XSS issue. In this example we have a WebView, which consists of a simple form with one input field. The form doesn't go anywhere, but if we insert `<script>alert("xss");</script>` and we get a popup, you can be pretty sure that you are open to XSS attack.

It's possible to add some JavaScript to gain access to shared preference files using the `file:///` command or use smsJSInterface.launchSMSActivity to send unwanted SMS messages from the phone.

If you turn off the `setJavaScriptEnabled` as follows, the alert will go away and nobody will be able to run any Javascript to perform XSS attacks:

```
myWebView.getSettings().setJavaScriptEnabled(false);
```

If this is not possible, then you can use an HTML encoding library such as the OWASP ESAPI library. See the XSS (Cross-Site Scripting) Prevention Cheat Sheet (www.owasp.org/index.php/XSS_(Cross_Site_Scripting)_Prevention_Cheat_Sheet) for more details and a list of ways to prevent XSS if you want to code it yourself.

Listing 6-6 XSS

```
package com.riis.xss;

import android.os.Bundle;
import android.annotation.SuppressLint;import android.app.Activity;
import android.util.Log;
import android.webkit.WebChromeClient;
import android.webkit.WebView;

public class MainActivity extends Activity {

    @SuppressLint("SetJavaScriptEnabled") @Override
    protected void onCreate(Bundle savedInstanceState) {
        super.onCreate(savedInstanceState);
        setContentView(R.layout.activity_main);

        WebView myWebView = (WebView) findViewById(R.id.webview);
        myWebView.getSettings().setJavaScriptEnabled(true);  // set to false to
        disable
        myWebView.setWebChromeClient(new WebChromeClient());

        String customHtml = "<html><body>";
        customHtml += "<form><input type=\"text\" name=\"xss\">";
        customHtml += "<input type=\"submit\"></form>";
        customHtml += "</body></html>";
```

```
        myWebView.loadData(customHtml, "text/html", "UTF-8");

        Log.d("com.riis.xss","customHTML is " + customHtml);

    }

}
```

Cloud

In this section, it's a case of what's old is new again. The same security best practices that have applied to web servers for the past twenty years apply to web servers used in mobile apps. Thankfully, there's another OWASP Web Top 10 list that we can use for help.

There can be some great benefits to using cloud storage given that someone else is taking care of a lot of the risks identified in the OWASP Web Top 10. However, there are other new concerns that are addressed in the OWASP Cloud Top 10.

OWASP Web Top 10 Risks

The OWASP Web Top 10 risks are described in the following sections.

A1. Injection

As noted previously, SQL injection involves changing the ID in the query string to see what you can find—for example, trying something like http://example.com /app/accountView?id=' or '1'='1 to see if the entire data set can be returned. A4 is also a type of injection, where we modify one of the IDs to see if that can return someone else's account data—for example, where http://example.com/app /accountView?id='123' is changed to http://example.com/app/accountView?id='124'.

A2. Broken Authentication and Session Management

Broken authentication and session management is a failure to secure logins by not protecting the username and passwords.

A3. Cross-Site Scripting

In the previous section we covered Cross-Site Scripting (XSS) and how it applies to Android in particular. But it can also apply to web pages hosted on a web server and loaded into the Android app.

A4. Insecure Direct Object References

Insecure Direct Object References occur when the value of an account (refer to Figure 6-5), invoice, or username can be accessed from a web service or query string. Rather than allowing direct access, the invoice or account number should be mapped indirectly to the actual number. Better still, don't use object references at all in your web service calls, although this may not be ideal if you're using RESTful APIs.

A5. Security Misconfiguration

Security misconfiguration basically involves making sure that all server software is up-to-date with the latest security patches; all the unnecessary ports, services, pages, and so forth are disabled via the firewall or server configuration; all default account passwords are changed or also disabled; and all development frameworks (Struts, ASP.Net, etc.) are secured. A good automated penetration-testing tool should be used to make sure the web server has all the latest patches.

A6. Sensitive Data Exposure

Sensitive data exposure means that your user's personal information is not secured correctly and can be seen by other users. This is typically SSNs or credit card numbers accessed in web user directories that have not been locked down.

A7. Missing Function-Level Access Control

This can mean different things for web servers, but for mobile apps the message is, first, that you should not rely on the client mobile app to provide the security. The back-end server should be checking for usernames and passwords or session tokens; otherwise, someone hitting the back-end server directly might be able to access customer information. Second, there shouldn't be any ability to gain access to any admin functionality by simply guessing the admin URL. Any additional privileges should only be available with a valid admin username and password.

A8. Cross-Site Request Forgery

Cross-site request forgery (CSRF) is an important concept for mobile apps. If the user's token is known, then it's possible to send the user an email or get him to click on a link in a web page so that he unintentionally performs an action on the back-end web server. Many apps store a user token in the shared preferences that can be obtained by backing up the user's data. Tokens should also be long and random so that there is no discernable pattern to each user's token.

A9. Using Components with Known Vulnerabilities

Similar to A5, unless you have someone scanning the security mailing lists and keeping all components on your web servers up to date, it makes sense to use an automated penetration-testing tool to alert you to any frameworks that may be vulnerable and open to attack.

A10. Unvalidated Redirects and Forwards

Avoid using redirects as they may be used to look for admin or other unauthorized pages. If you're using OAuth, the redirect URLs are known and should be added to a whitelist, and all other redirects should be ignored.

OWASP Cloud Top 10 Risks

The OWASP Cloud Top 10 risks are described in the following sections.

R2. Accountability & Data Risk

More and more, enterprises are moving away from company-owned data centers and servers. If your data is in the cloud, then know who has access to the data and where the data is stored.   Companies outside of the United States are now asking for cloud storage somewhere besides the United States because they are worried the NSA might be spying on them. Companies in the United States don't want their data stored in European data centers because they don't want to be subject to EU data protection laws.

R2. User Identity Federation

Use Security Assertion Markup Language (SAML) between different cloud providers for a better user experience. SAML is a single sign-on framework for passing credentials between systems. It is important for the enterprises to keep control over user identities as they move services and applications to the different cloud providers. Rather than letting cloud providers create multiple islands of identities that become too complex to manage down the line, enterprises should federate the UserIDs using LDAP or Active Directory.

R3. Regulatory Compliance

As mentioned in R1, different countries have different compliance rules and you should be aware of them. You also need to ensure that your data is HIPPA/SOX compliant where applicable. Data that is perceived to be secure in one country may not be perceived as secure in another due to different regulatory laws across countries or regions. For instance, the European Union has very strict privacy laws, and hence data stored in United States may not comply with those EU laws.

R4. Business Continuity & Resiliency

Cloud storage does fail from time to time, so be sure you have service-level agreements and quality of service agreements in place if your app needs to be up 24/7. Also, make sure that your provider has a disaster recovery plan if something does fail.

R5. User Privacy & Secondary Usage of Data

Make sure your provider has a privacy policy and won't use your customer data for other purposes. Make sure your cloud provider knows what data can or cannot be used by them for secondary purposes. This includes data that can be mined directly from user data by providers or indirectly based on user behavior (clicks, incoming/outgoing URLs, etc.).

R6. Service & Data Integration

Any data transferred between the end user and the cloud data center should be encrypted. Any data transferred between different cloud servers should also be encrypted using SFTP.

R7. Multi-tenancy & Physical Security

Are you sharing a physical machine with other customers of the cloud provider? If so, how is the data logically and physically segregated between customers? Is it possible for someone else to inadvertently see your data? Do other customers have physical access to the data center machines?

R8. Incidence Analysis & Forensics

If there is a break-in, are the audit trails and logs segregated for better forensics or are they mixed with other customers' data?

R9. Infrastructure Security

One of the major benefits of putting your web services or server in the cloud is that someone else can take care of the security patches that need to be applied to the web server, application servers, routers, firewalls, and so on. But there's an assumption that the cloud provider is following its own best practices. Read the provider's policy and process documentation, and request recent third-party risk assessments. The provider must be willing to supply this.

R10. Non-production Environment Exposure

If you are using test and development servers in the cloud, there is a much higher risk that information can be stolen from these traditionally less-secure environments. Don't use old production data on test servers.

HIPAA Web Server Compliance

In Chapter 1 we covered HIPAA requirements for mobile apps. HIPAA is much different from other security lists as there is considerable focus on auditing and reporting break-ins. Logging on the client is insecure and cannot be relied on. Logging events, actions, and web server requests on the server are essential for HIPAA compliance and follow-up if there has been a security leak of any personal information on a healthcare app.

HIPAA-compliant web servers need to provide the following security measures:

- Third-party HIPAA compliance assessment
- HIPAA-compliant employee controls for both physical and electronic access

- Third-party facilities and data center audits
- Vulnerability scans for risk analysis
- Data encryption for data in motion and at rest
- Encrypted offsite data backups
- Device and media controls for media disposal and media re-use
- Multi-factor authentication support
- Application access controls

You may decide that you need to move to a cloud provider for your HIPAA cloud data. You, as the HIPAA-compliant hospital or physician's office, also known as a Covered Entity, need to extend this to the cloud provider. As part of the contract process you will need to make sure that the cloud provider signs what is known as a Business Associate Agreement (BAA). With a BAA the cloud provider becomes an extension of the Covered Entity. This also impacts liability issues and can protect you from many of the HIPAA fines should any web server data leaks occur, as these may be passed on to the cloud provider.

Conclusion

In this chapter we've looked at how to protect the other half of your mobile application, namely the back-end web server. We've looked at web service attacks and learned just how much a server should trust its incoming requests. We have examined the very different types of attacks that cross-platform and hybrid apps should expect, such as XSS and SQL injection; how you should sanitize untrusted data before executing; and how you should use prepared SQL statements rather than concatenating strings to build your SQL query. We've learned why you should disable JavaScript in WebView where possible. Finally, we've looked at what decisions you should make when you choose a cloud provider if you're putting your web server in the cloud.

7

Third-Party Library Integration

Third-party libraries are part and parcel of Android development. Whether it's adding Crittercism, AdMob, Relic, or some open source libraries such as ZXing or UIL, these are typically added to your app to create a better user experience. The truth is that you probably don't know in detail what code is doing or how it is doing it.

There are many reasons why you might want to add a third-party SDK to your APK. Typically you do it for one of the following reasons, although admittedly this is only a very limited list:

- Selling banner adverts
- Collecting users' analytics
- Collecting crash report information
- Speech recognition
- Photo editing
- 3D imaging
- Taking payments

With only a few notable exceptions, these are added to your project during development as a jar file. Most also need one or two modifications to your AndroidManifest .xml and your onCreate() method.

A few others have Eclipse or Android Studio plug-ins that will add the files and instrument your code for you. This makes it very easy to add, for example, defect tracking to your app.

However, there's a level of trust here that as yet hasn't been earned. It is much better to take a "trust but verify" approach to any third-party APKs you're using to make sure you're not sending back more user information to these third-party services than you expected to send.

Be especially careful of any post-processing tools, because whatever you're gaining in ease of use you almost certainly are giving up in visibility.

There have been a number of examples in the past when third-party advertising services were pulling location and device IDs from phones without the developer or user's knowledge. But as a developer, pleading ignorance is not going to help if your HIPAA-compliant APK is found to be leaking personal health information (PHI).

In this chapter we'll look at some strategies for protecting your users from any third-party SDK trickery. This isn't only limited to third-party SDKs; it also applies to any third-party contractors, vendors, or offshore development houses. It's in your interest to know how to check your code.

If your app is using any open source libraries or you are reusing code from a different app, then it's still your responsibility to make sure that whatever code is shipped with your APK is not collecting more user information than the bare minimum required to make the APK fully functional.

Transferring the Risk

Most Android apps include code that is reused or outsourced, or that contains third-party libraries. These libraries are distributed, often in binary format, or sometimes they come with the source code. But other than the vendors or open source developers, nobody really knows exactly what the code does.

There is a level of trust that occurs whereby a developer assumes that the code is not taking advantage of you as the developer and, ultimately, your users.

Over the last few years there have been a number of newspaper articles about third-party apps being responsible for unauthorized transmissions of a user's location information (see Figure 7-1 for an article about AdMob collecting location information from Pandora users).

In most cases it's not the third-party library that the articles focus on, but it's the app they get delivered in that gets the brunt of the bad publicity.

Permissions

In most cases third-party libraries can't collect extra data without asking for the appropriate permissions because of the design of the Android framework. If the third-party app is looking for any of the following, you should be sure there is a good reason for the request:

- ACCESS_COARSE_LOCATION
- ACCESS_FINE_LOCATION
- BLUETOOTH_ADMIN
- BLUETOOTH_PRIVILEGED
- CALL_PHONE

TECHNOLOGY

Mobile-App Makers Face U.S. Privacy Investiga

✉ Email   🖶 Print   💬 27 Comments   [f] [y] [N+] [in]   A   A

By AMIR EFRATI, SCOTT THURM and DIONNE SEARCEY

Updated April 5, 2011 8:06 a.m. ET

Federal prosecutors in New Jersey are investigating whether numerous smartphone applications illegally obtained or transmitted information about their users without proper disclosures, according to a person familiar with the matter.

Online-music streaming service Pandora, which plans an initial public offering, says in an SEC filing that it has been subpoenaed in an investigation probing information-sharing by mobile applications. John Letzing and Stacey Delo discuss.

The criminal investigation is examining whether the app makers fully described to users the types of data they collected and why they needed the information—such as a user's location or a unique identifier for the phone—the person familiar with the matter said. Collecting information about a user without proper notice or authorization could violate a federal computer-fraud law.

Online music service Pandora Media Inc. said Monday it received a subpoena related to a federal grand-jury investigation of information-sharing practices by smartphone applications.

Pandora disclosed the subpoena, issued "in early 2011," in a Securities and Exchange Commission filing. The Oakland, Calif., company said it had been informed it is "not a specific target of the investigation." Pandora said it believed similar subpoenas had been

Figure 7-1   Pandora and AdMob hack

- CAMERA
- INTERNET
- READ_CALENDAR
- READ_CONTACTS
- READ_INPUT_STATE
- READ_SMS
- READ_SOCIAL_STREAM

- RECEIVE_MMS
- RECEIVE_SMS
- RECORD_AUDIO
- SEND_SMS
- WRITE_CALENDAR
- WRITE_CONTACTS
- WRITE_SMS
- WRITE_SOCIAL_STREAM

Because of bad publicity in the past, some users are aware that asking for any of these permissions without a reason is going to have an impact on your app reviews.

Next, let's look at a couple of third-party SDKs to see how they're installed, to make sure you're aware of just what you're agreeing to when you add them to your code.

Installing Third-Party Apps

Installing third-party apps will help you understand what we may be opening ourselves up to from privacy and security perspectives. We'll look at two defect-tracking apps, Crittercism and Crashlytics.

Installing Crittercism

Take the following steps to install Critercism.

1. Create an account on Crittercism.

2. Register the app on the Crittercism site.

3. Download the SDK.

4. Copy the Crittercism JAR file to your libs folder.

5. If you're using Eclipse, right-click your project, click Properties, select Java Build Path, click Add External Jar, and then add the Crittercism JAR file.

6. Add the following line to your AndroidManifest.xml file:

   ```
   <uses-permission android:name="android.permission.INTERNET"/>
   ```

7. Add the Crittercism import and the app Id (see lines 10 and 22 in Listing 7-1). You can find the app id for your app in the query string of Crittercism's app manager (see Figure 7-2).

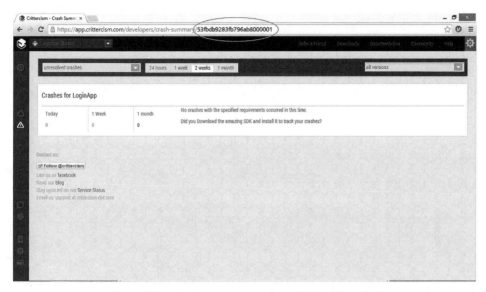

Figure 7-2 Crittercism app manager with AppID circled

Listing 7-1   **LoginApp with Crittercism**

```
package com.riis.logincrittercism;

import com.riis.logincrittercism.R;

import android.os.Bundle;
import android.app.Activity;
import android.view.View;
import android.widget.Button;
import android.widget.EditText;
import com.crittercism.app.Crittercism;                      //line 10


public class LoginActivity extends Activity {

  private Button loginButton;

    @Override
    protected void onCreate(Bundle savedInstanceState) {
        super.onCreate(savedInstanceState);
        setContentView(R.layout.login _ screen);
                                                        // line 21
        Crittercism.initialize(getApplicationContext(), "53fbdb9283fb796ab8000001");

        initializeViews();
        bindListenersToViews();

    }
```

```
private void initializeViews() {
    loginButton = (Button) findViewById(R.id.login_button);

}

  private void bindListenersToViews() {
      loginButton.setOnClickListener(new View.OnClickListener() {
          @Override
          public void onClick(View v) {
                  loginToApp();
          }
  });
}

  private void loginToApp() {
      EditText usernameField = (EditText) findViewById(R.id.username_field);
      EditText passwordField = (EditText) findViewById(R.id.password_field);
      EditText emailField = (EditText) findViewById(R.id.email_field);


      if(areFieldsEmpty(usernameField, passwordField, emailField)) {
              AlertDialogs.showEmptyFieldsAlertDialog(this);
              return;
      }
  }

  private boolean areFieldsEmpty(EditText... fields) {
      for(int i = 0; i < fields.length; i++) {
              if(fields[i].getText().toString().matches("")) {
                      return true;
              }
      }

      return false;
  }

}
```

The app is now ready to build. Information will begin showing up in the app manager when it starts generating some traffic from all those downloads on Google Play or even if it's installed directly onto a device using adb install. This is obviously a very hands-on approach.

In this example we see that it's asking for an INTERNET permission. Although it's in our list of dangerous permissions, Crittercism needs it to collect crash reports, so it's okay to include it in your AndroidManifest.xml file. You should not install any SDK that asks for permissions that it doesn't need to perform its core functionality, and thankfully the Crittercism SDK is not asking for any other permissions, such as location or camera.

Installing Crashlytics

With Crittercism, it's obvious just what it is doing to your app. Crashlytics, however, installs as a plug-in, and with plug-ins and other automated installs you need to be aware of just what is happening to your code. Because of their ease of use, the temptation is to simply ignore what they're doing. Trust but verify all third-party SDKs, code, and open source libraries that you add to your code. Typically there isn't anything to worry about with these tools, such as Crashlytics, but you need to know how to be sure no information is being leaked, because ultimately you are responsible for the security of your users.

If you're using Eclipse, go to Help->Install New Software and enter https://crashlytics.com/download/eclipse in the Work With section. Then the wizard will walk you through how to install Crashlytics.

Once Eclipse restarts, Crashlytics will be installed on the toolbar. Click the red icon on the Eclipse toolbar (see Figure 7-3) and it will add it to your chosen project.

The Crashlytics wizard adds the SDK to your app. We can see the changes to the LoginActivity code in Listing 7-2, which shows the imported classes on line 3 and the inserted `Crashlytics.start(this);` on line 19.

Listing 7-2   **LoginApp with Crashylitics**

```
package com.riis.logincrashlytics;

import com.crashlytics.android.Crashlytics;      // line 3
import com.riis.logincrashlytics.R;

import android.os.Bundle;
import android.app.Activity;
import android.view.View;
import android.widget.Button;
import android.widget.EditText;

public class LoginActivity extends Activity {

  private Button loginButton;

    @Override
    protected void onCreate(Bundle savedInstanceState) {
        super.onCreate(savedInstanceState);
        Crashlytics.start(this);                 // line 19
        setContentView(R.layout.login _ screen);

        initializeViews();
        bindListenersToViews();

    }
```

Figure 7-3   Adding Crashlytics to an app

```java
private void initializeViews() {
    loginButton = (Button) findViewById(R.id.login_button);

}

  private void bindListenersToViews() {
      loginButton.setOnClickListener(new View.OnClickListener() {
          @Override
          public void onClick(View v) {
                  loginToApp();
          }
   });
  }

  private void loginToApp() {
      EditText usernameField = (EditText) findViewById(R.id.username_field);
      EditText passwordField = (EditText) findViewById(R.id.password_field);
      EditText emailField = (EditText) findViewById(R.id.email_field);


      if(areFieldsEmpty(usernameField, passwordField, emailField)) {
              AlertDialogs.showEmptyFieldsAlertDialog(this);
              return;
      }
  }

  private boolean areFieldsEmpty(EditText... fields) {
      for(int i = 0; i < fields.length; i++) {
```

```
                if(fields[i].getText().toString().matches("")) {
                        return true;
                }
        }

        return false;
    }

}
```

The AndroidManifest.xml file (see Listing 7-3), just like Crittercism, adds the INTERNET permission as well as an API key on line 27.

Listing 7-3 **AndroidManifest.xml**

```xml
<?xml version="1.0" encoding="utf-8"?>
<manifest xmlns:android="http://schemas.android.com/apk/res/android"
    package="com.riis.logincrashlytics"
    android:versionCode="1"
    android:versionName="1.0" >

    <uses-sdk
        android:minSdkVersion="8"
        android:targetSdkVersion="18" />

    <uses-permission android:name="android.permission.INTERNET"/>        //line 11

    <application
        android:allowBackup="true"
        android:icon="@drawable/ic_launcher"
        android:label="@string/app_name"
        android:theme="@style/AppTheme" >
        <activity
            android:name="com.riis.logincrashlytics.LoginActivity"
            android:label="@string/app_name" >
            <intent-filter>
                <action android:name="android.intent.action.MAIN" />

                <category android:name="android.intent.category.LAUNCHER" />
            </intent-filter>
        </activity>
        <meta-data android:name="com.crashlytics.ApiKey" android:value="aad91e5bd965
        d05ab60803fe528ee70725ff6102"/>                    //line 27
    </application>

</manifest>
```

Crashlytics is so easy to use that it would be easy to click the wizard and not pay much attention to the man behind the red icon. In this case there is nothing to worry about.

> **Note**
>
> When using automated tools such as Crashlytics, check your code into your favorite source code repository before running the tool, and then check it in again after the changes to quickly see what has changed in your project code.

Trust but Verify

Let's assume you install the SDK and the list of permissions makes sense. Is there anything else that can go wrong? Unfortunately, there may still be cause for concern. You are still the developer or company that is ultimately assuming the risk for any data leakage. You need to perform more due diligence and check to see whether the SDK is collecting other data to send back to its servers. We can do this in a couple of ways: (1) by searching a decompiled version of the library for suspicious strings or by searching the original codebase if it's open source, or (2) by trying to use a man-in-the-middle attack to see how the data is being transmitted across the network.

Decompiling SDKs

You can decompile the SDK's library jar file after you download the SDK using the JD-GUI decompiler. Alternatively, if the SDK is already in your app, take the following steps that are similar to what we've already covered in earlier chapters, although this time you don't need to pull the APK off the device. You need to export it to the filesystem:

1. Build using your favorite IDE.

2. Export your APK; if you're using Eclipse, right-click on the project and choose Android Tools->Export Unsigned Package.

3. dex2jar your APK. See Chapter 1 if you need to review how to do this.

4. Open the apk_de2jar.jar file in JD-GUI.

After you have the source code in JD-GUI, search for the following strings to see whether there is any extra user or device data being collected. You should add more to this list for your own purposes:

- getDeviceID
- android_id
- device_id

- TelephonyManager
- Location
- getLatitude
- getLongitude
- getLastKnownLocation
- android.provider.ContactsContract
- sms or content://sms/
- setCamera
- MediaRecorder

Figure 7-4 shows location-gathering information in the MobClix SDK.

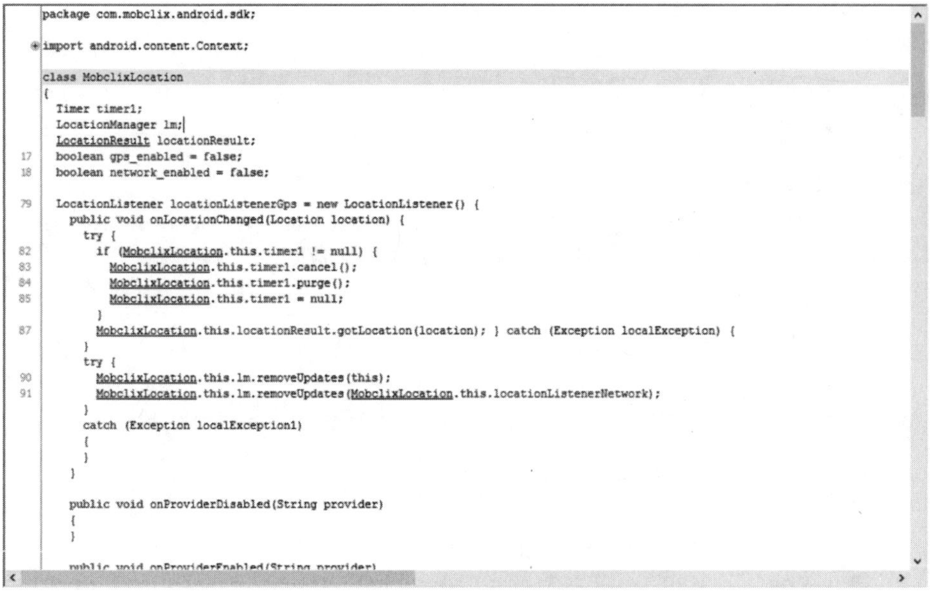

```
package com.mobclix.android.sdk;

import android.content.Context;

class MobclixLocation
{
  Timer timer1;
  LocationManager lm;
  LocationResult locationResult;
17  boolean gps_enabled = false;
18  boolean network_enabled = false;

79  LocationListener locationListenerGps = new LocationListener() {
      public void onLocationChanged(Location location) {
        try {
82          if (MobclixLocation.this.timer1 != null) {
83            MobclixLocation.this.timer1.cancel();
84            MobclixLocation.this.timer1.purge();
85            MobclixLocation.this.timer1 = null;
          }
87          MobclixLocation.this.locationResult.gotLocation(location); } catch (Exception localException) {
        }
        try {
90          MobclixLocation.this.lm.removeUpdates(this);
91          MobclixLocation.this.lm.removeUpdates(MobclixLocation.this.locationListenerNetwork);
        }
        catch (Exception localException1)
        {
        }
      }

      public void onProviderDisabled(String provider)
      {
      }

      public void onProviderEnabled(String provider)
```

Figure 7-4   Location information

Figure 7-5 shows Millennial Media asking for the device's android_id.

Figure 7-6 shows some `getDeviceID` calls from an SDK within an APK—we used Ticketmaster as our example—that calls `getDeviceID()`. This is also obfuscated, which is not uncommon in third-party SDKs.

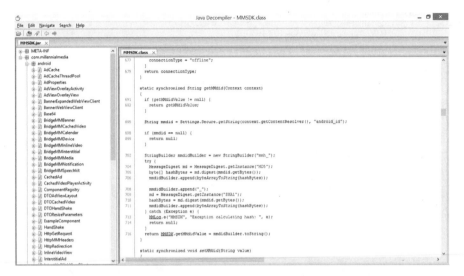

Figure 7-5   Reading android_id

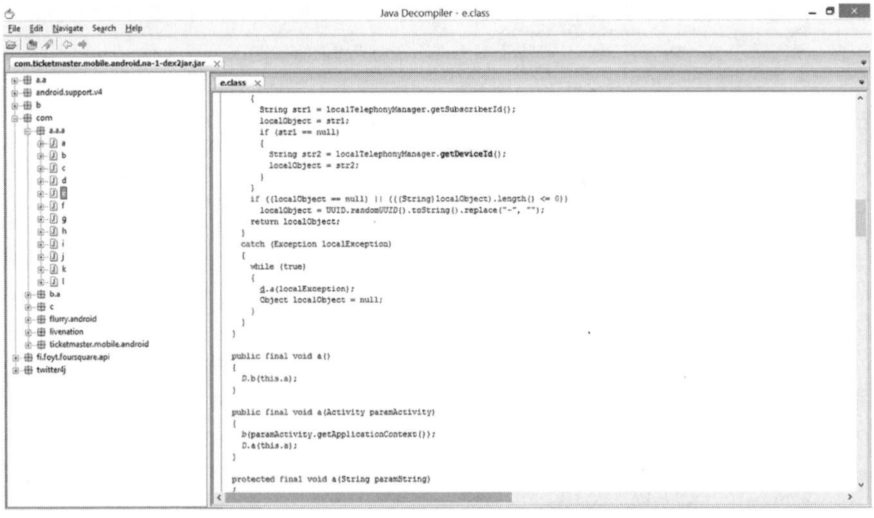

Figure 7-6   `getDeviceID` calls

As we can clearly see, the code and most examples we've shown are not obfuscated at time of printing. So you should also be able to see whether the third-party SDK is trying to do any of the following as part of your due diligence:

- Reading phone state and device identity
- Modifying global system settings
- Preventing device from going to sleep
- Changing wi-fi state
- Changing network connectivity
- Automatically starting the app on boot
- Creating Bluetooth connections
- Viewing network state
- Viewing wi-fi state
- Reading contact data
- Adding or modifying calendar events
- Sending emails

Man in the Middle

Earlier in this book, in Chapter 4, we looked at how hackers can use man-in-the-middle attacks (MITM) to capture your login credentials, API keys, and other personal information via a proxy. We can try to do the same to make sure that third-party SDKs are reporting data back to the server securely. Ideally we'd want to make sure the app is sending things back to the third-party back-end servers using HTTPS. Figure 7-7 shows an example of an app that looks like it was built for collecting information and, worse still, is communicating insecurely over HTTP.

Figure 7-8 shows a screen capture of Charles Proxy running a number of test apps and commercial apps on a device. All of these third-party SDKs are using HTTPS and not HTTP, so there is little to see here except for some Google Analytics, which suggests the apps are sending back what you would expect.

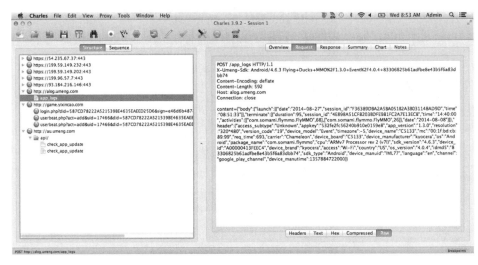

Figure 7-7   MITM attack on Flying Ducks Android App

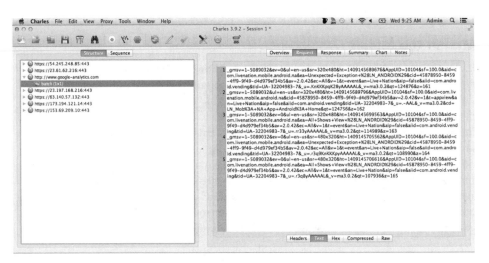

Figure 7-8   MITM on third-party SDKs

Conclusion

In this chapter we talked about how the developer of an app is ultimately the person responsible for the user's security and privacy regardless of what third-party code ends up in your APK. To help you assume the risk with a lot more confidence, in the rest of the chapter we looked at what to look for when you're installing a third-party SDK. We also showed how to look at the original code and what strings and functionality to search for when you're doing your due diligence. Finally, we used Charles Proxy to see how third-party SDKs were sending back information to their web servers. The SDKs were using SSL to transmit the data, which makes the data secure and hidden away from prying eyes.

8

Device Security

Many of the security issues we've seen in this book are limited to a single device, such as the many examples of usernames and passwords or credit card information stored in the shared preferences on the device. There is no malware app—as yet—that, once it has been downloaded, targets an exploit to collect mass quantities of these usernames and passwords from a specific app with a known problem. For this to succeed, the shared preferences file or database would also have to be created as `world_readable`, which is not the default way to output to a file or SQLite database, so it's unlikely but not impossible. It's a very good reason to not root your phone in case some app uses root to gain access to those files.

These examples of personal information leakage would in no way be HIPAA compliant. But in most cases, to gain access to your unprotected app data someone would need to connect a user's tablet or phone to a computer via a USB to back up the data—and only then if it was running a specific version of the Android OS. The argument we've heard many times is that it's unlikely someone will gain access to the device for long enough to be able to back up an app's data.

However, according to Avast, more than 80,000 used cell phones are for sale online through eBay and other online auction sites every day, and the majority have not been wiped correctly (http://blog.avast.com/2014/07/08/tens-of-thousands-of-americans-sell-themselves-online-every-day/).

If you are looking at app security holistically, it's important to assume that multiple people are going to have access to a device over its lifetime and that it will not be adequately wiped each time. These used phones can also be rooted, meaning you cannot assume that setting `allowBackup=false` is going to be enough to guarantee that the data is not going to be found. Corporate users will need to take extra precautions to ensure that company data is not compromised.

Android security also doesn't just depend on your secure coding practices. It also depends on the underlying version of the Android OS. For example, we've used the adb backup command many times in the book so far on a non-rooted phone, but there are other security issues you should know about that may have implications for your security. We'll look at these device security issues and more in this chapter.

Wiping Your Device

To safely wipe your Android phone, take the following steps:

1. Encrypt your phone. See the "Device Encryption" section later in this chapter.

2. Perform a Factory data reset by going to Settings->Backup & Reset->Factory Data Reset and reset your phone.

3. Load some fake contacts and pictures.

4. Perform a Factory data reset again.

Fragmentation

Fragmentation is huge from a developer's perspective. With approximately 20,000 different devices, how do you know what to test to make sure your app's functionality works across every device? And fragmentation also comes in two flavors, software and hardware. Most devices will support multiple versions of the Android software or OS. Each version of the Android OS gets more and more secure, but there are still lots of earlier versions of the OS being used every day in the wild (see Figure 8-1 for the latest figures for Android) that are not as secure as KitKat.

In the past, carriers were reluctant to upgrade to newer, more secure versions, but this is changing, especially for the bigger carriers in the United States (see www.androidcentral.com/tag/ota for a list of Over the Air (OTA) updates in the last couple of years). If you want the latest version of Android available for your device, go to Settings->About Device and click on Software update to get the latest version available.

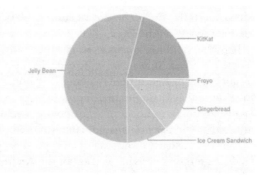

Version	Codename	API	Distribution
2.2	Froyo	8	0.7%
2.3.3 - 2.3.7	Gingerbread	10	13.6%
4.0.3 - 4.0.4	Ice Cream Sandwich	15	10.6%
4.1.x	Jelly Bean	16	26.5%
4.2.x		17	19.8%
4.3		18	7.9%
4.4	KitKat	19	20.9%

Figure 8-1   OS dashboard

adb Backup

The adb backup command, which we've used a number of times in this book to retrieve an APK's real-time stored data, was first introduced in Android 4.0 or Ice Cream Sandwich. It also works with earlier versions of Jelly Bean, so if you're using Android 4.0 or above you can back up app data without being rooted. Before adb backup you could pull individual files using adb pull, but more often than not the phone had to be rooted and the permissions changed to get at the file. adb backup made this so much easier: In one command all the files in the /data/data folder for that APK or all APKs were backed up onto a remote computer in a Unix tar-like format. We can see from Figure 8-1 that the majority of Android phones suffer from this problem.

You can explicitly turn off Android Backups by setting android:allowBackup="false" in the application attribute in the AndroidManifest.xml file. But this solution has only limited security given that a rooted device will still allow access to these files. As discussed, there are so many secondhand phones on the market these days that you should assume that, sooner or later, someone is going to have access to the phone and more than enough time to get at your files.

Logs

It's common to add debug logging information to an app when it's being developed. Unfortunately, many of these debug logs make it into production.

To see all of the logging information, simply type adb logcat from the command line. There is such a wealth of information that it helps to save it out to a file using adb logcat > logging.txt to get some idea of what's in the logs.

We can filter the logs using LogCat that can be run from the command line. LogCat also comes with the Dalvik Debug Monitor Server (DDMS) that is part of the Android SDK. Ideally, because of the volume of logs, we'd want to filter the logs based on log messages coming from the application we're looking at. See Figure 8-2 for the log messages from com.riis.logfiles.

However, what we don't want to do is leak any personal information via logging, or log what http calls we're making so others can see how you're talking to the back end. Up to Android 4.1.x or Jelly Bean, there were no restrictions on what logs an Android app could read. Now an app can only read logs that it wrote and not logs written by other apps. The highlighted line in Figure 8-2 shows that we're logging passport information.

The example comes from a real-world app, in this case a major airline that was logging a customer's passport number after that customer bought an international ticket on the mobile app. If that was running on the approximately 25 percent of devices running something earlier than Android Jelly Bean, another Android app could read and harvest those passport numbers.

Listing 8-1 contains the code for our simple demo to show how logs can leak information. Normally we'd be logging the passport number after the user has entered the

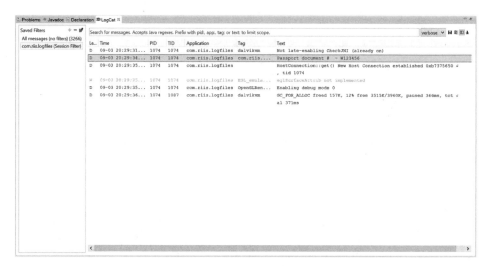

Figure 8-2   Logfiles before ProGuard

data, but we're going to hard code it here for demonstration purposes. If you run the app, you can see the logs in logcat, similar to Figure 8-2.

Listing 8-1   **Logging passport numbers**

```
package com.riis.logfiles;

import android.os.Bundle;
import android.util.Log;
import android.app.Activity;

public class MainActivity extends Activity {

    public static final String APP_TAG = "com.riis.logfiles";
    public static final String PassportNumber = "W123456";

    @Override
    protected void onCreate(Bundle savedInstanceState) {
        super.onCreate(savedInstanceState);
        setContentView(R.layout.activity_main);

        // todo - add code to enter passport number

        Log.d(APP_TAG, "Passport document #  - " + PassportNumber);

    }

}
```

Listing 8-2 contains the code to read the log information from a different app. It simply collects all the logs after running the logcat command but filters or targets the debug messages from our com.riis.logfiles app using the command `logcat -d com.riis.logfiles:D *:S`. This app requires the user to agree to the following permission, android.permission.READ_LOGS, which might or might not raise a red flag.

Listing 8-2   **Read logs**

```
package com.riis.readlogs;

import java.io.BufferedReader;
import java.io.IOException;
import java.io.InputStreamReader;

import android.os.Bundle;
import android.app.Activity;
import android.util.Log;

public class MainActivity extends Activity {
    public static final String APP_TAG = "com.riis.readlogs";

    @Override
    protected void onCreate(Bundle savedInstanceState) {
        super.onCreate(savedInstanceState);
        setContentView(R.layout.activity_main);

        try {
                Process process = Runtime.getRuntime().exec("logcat -d com.riis.
                logfiles:D *:S");
                BufferedReader bufferedReader = new BufferedReader(
                new InputStreamReader(process.getInputStream()));

                StringBuilder log=new StringBuilder();
                String line = "";
                while ((line = bufferedReader.readLine()) != null) {
                  log.append(line);
                }
                Log.d(APP_TAG, log.toString());

        }
        catch (IOException e)
        {
            // todo
        }


    }

}
```

Ideally we would remove all logging code and not ship the app with any debugging information. Usually the ProGuard tool is used to obfuscate your code, but we can also use ProGuard to remove all logs in our production apps. To turn on ProGuard, first comment out the ProGuard configuration line in the project.properties file. This will rename the strings in a file to short characters and generally make it more difficult to understand. But we can also strip out methods. Add the code in Listing 8-3 to the proguard-project.txt configuration file and it will strip the logging code from the production app. Chapter 2 explained how to do this in Android Studio.

Listing 8-3   **Remove logs**

```
-assumenosideeffects class android.util.Log {
    <methods>;
}
```

We have to create a production APK for ProGuard to kick in, which means we have to run it differently in Eclipse. Click on Export signed app and walk through the wizard. You'll need a keyfile before you do this. Make sure the file has been obfuscated by decompiling it using dex2jar and jd-gui (see Chapter 2 for the steps). Now see whether it sends any logging information when it's on the device. First, use the adb install command to install the production APK, and then use logcat to see what information is being logged. As you can see in Figure 8-3, the passport information is no longer sent to the log even though the Java code has not been changed.

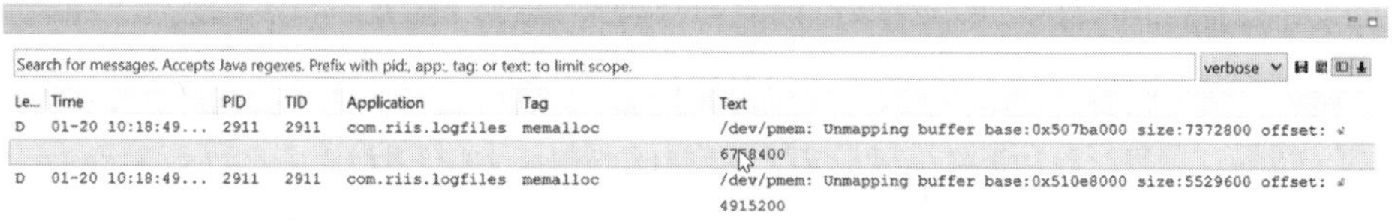

Figure 8-3   Logfiles after ProGuard

Device Encryption

If you're working with a limited audience of users, such as for an internal corporate app, and these users can live with reboot times reminiscent of Windows Vista, then you might want to consider turning on encryption for the devices. Currently, this will probably only be acceptable to users who value their security more than their time. Though not confirmed yet, it is rumored that all devices will be encrypted by default in the next version of the OS, Android L (see www.washingtonpost.com/blogs /the-switch/wp/2014/09/18/newest-androids-will-join-iphones-in-offering-default-encryption-blocking-police/).

The downside is that the speed to restart your phone is longer and that you need to enter a password or PIN every time the phone is rebooted. The upside is that the /data/data and /data/app folders are encrypted if the phone is lost. And if you're storing Protected Health Information (PHI) on the device, HIPAA requires that this data be encrypted.

To enable encryption on a Samsung S4, take the following steps.

1. Plug in your device's charger and keep it connected during the process.

2. Go to Settings->More->Security and tap Encrypt device.

3. Select the Screen Lock menu item and choose a PIN or Password as your encryption key, as shown in Figure 8-4. Go with a longer password and follow the prompts to confirm it as a four-digit PIN can be bypassed using a brute-force attack.

4. Press the Encrypt phone or Encrypt tablet button.

5. The device will reboot several times during the encryption process, which can take 30 minutes or more.

6. Enter your PIN or password.

Other phones have different ways of getting to their settings:

- In the LG (L34C): Settings -> Security -> Encrypt Phone
- In a HTC (one M8): Settings -> Storage -> Phone Storage Encryption
- In a Nexus 7 (Nexus 7-2012): Settings-> Security -> Encrypt Tablet

As a side note to the previous section on fragmentation, it's worth mentioning that there is a freezer hack that can recover the encryption password that so far only works on Android 4.0.x. The attack involves putting the phone in a freezer, which allows the forensic tool enough time to read the encryption key in memory as it reboots (see https://www1.informatik.uni-erlangen.de/frost for more information). The irony, of course, is that this only works on Ice Cream Sandwich.

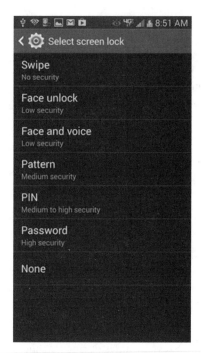

Figure 8-4   Encryption choices

SEAndroid

The NSA created SEAndroid as an attempt to "Identify and address critical gaps in the security of Android." Just as Android is a version of Linux, so too is SEAndroid a subset or version of SELinux.

SEAndroid is an extra layer of security on top of the Android Framework that prevents malware from gaining access to the framework. Any access to certain Android components is under the control of SEAndroid, meaning there are less likely to be root exploits. It is also going to be a better way to ensure separation between apps.

Android and Linux use a system known as Discretionary Access Control (DAC) that allows access based on the user's identity. SEAndroid extends this to Mandatory Access Control (MAC) and limits a user's privileges to processes and objects such as files, devices, and so forth.

SEAndroid enhances the Android system by doing the following:

- Confines privileged daemons to protect them from misuse
- Sandboxes and isolates apps from each other and from the system

- Prevents privilege escalation by apps
- Allows application privileges to be controlled at installation and runtime using Middleware Mandatory Access Control (MMAC)
- Provides a centralized, analyzable policy

At the moment these policies are created by the device manufacturer and currently only operate on Android system-level processes. But the good news is that these policies are now enforced in Android 4.4 (KitKat).

Currently, SEAndroid is not really a part of the developer's toolbox, but expect it to play a part in delivering secure apps to your enterprise as new versions of the Android OS are released.

We can already see some developments that are moving in that general direction. Samsung's Knox (see Figure 8-5), which is available on most Samsung devices, enables complete separation of the user's personal and corporate data by using two different profiles on the same device. Depending on the time of day, you can use the phone for business needs, with separate Knox apps and email configuration, and then later in the day you can use it for more personal apps and the like. If you leave your job, the corporate data can be wiped remotely without losing any pictures or personal emails.

Figure 8-5   Samsung Knox

FIPS 140-2

If your app needs to communicate with the US government or Department of Defense, any hardware and software you use needs to be FIPS 140-2 validated. FIPS stands for the Federal Information Processing Standards and 140-2 is the second version of the Security Requirements for Cryptographic Modules standard.

The standard defines 4 levels of FIPS 140-2, which are as follows:

- Level 1, the lowest, imposes very limited requirements; loosely, all components must be "production grade" and various egregious kinds of insecurity must be absent.

- Level 2 adds requirements for physical tamper-evidence and role-based authentication.

- Level 3 adds requirements for physical tamper resistance (making it difficult for attackers to gain access to sensitive information contained in the module) and identity-based authentication, and for a physical or logical separation between the interfaces by which "critical security parameters" enter and leave the module and its other interfaces.

- Level 4 makes the physical security requirements more stringent and requires robustness against environmental attacks.

A list of all the FIPS 140-2 validated hardware and software can be found at http://csrc.nist.gov/groups/STM/cmvp/documents/140-1/140val-all.htm.

A few devices, such as the Samsung S5, S4, and Note, as well as Motorola Droids and Moto G/X, have been validated to Level 1.

For cryptographic libraries there are a number of options. One of these, the OpenSSL FIPS library, provides a compliant C++ library. OpenSSL's FIPS module can be used with the help of NDK, and instructions on how to build it can be found at http://wiki.openssl.org/index.php/FIPS_Library_and_Android. There are also commercial libraries such as BSAFE and Mocana.

If you want to go through the process of getting your own Crypto software validated against the standard, you can find the complete standard at http://csrc.nist.gov/publications/fips/fips140-2/fips1402.pdf.

FIPS 140 imposes requirements in eleven different areas:

1. Cryptographic module specification (what must be documented)

2. Cryptographic module ports and interfaces (what information flows in and out, and how it must be segregated)

3. Roles, services, and authentication (who can do what with the module, and how this is checked)

4. Finite state model (documentation of the high-level states the module can be in, and how transitions occur)

5. Physical security (tamper evidence and resistance, and robustness against extreme environmental conditions)

6. Operational environment (what sort of operating system the module uses and is used by)

7. Cryptographic key management (generation, entry, output, storage, and destruction of keys)

8. EMI/EMC

9. Self-tests (what must be tested and when, and what must be done if a test fails)

10. Design assurance (what documentation must be provided to demonstrate that the module has been well designed and implemented)

11. Mitigation of other attacks (if a module is designed to mitigate against, say, TEMPEST attacks, then its documentation must say how)

Information on how the validation works can be found at http://csrc.nist.gov /groups/STM/cmvp/inprocess.html.

Mobile Device Management

Mobile Device Management (MDM) tools are used for managing devices in an enterprise, what are known as BYOD (Bring Your Own Device). MDM is now a multi-billion-dollar industry, and there are some more mature products out there that will help you manage employees' devices in a consistent way across your enterprise.

Figure 8-6 shows a list of devices that are being managed using VMware's MDM solution, AirWatch.

BYODs provide some obvious benefits:

- Central management of employee- and employer-purchased devices
- Ability to find and wipe devices remotely
- Ability to set up KNOX-like sandboxes to firewall company documents
- Controlled access to internal networks
- Improved productivity and ease of use

However, it is not all good news. Do not assume your MDM deployment is secure. There are many examples out there where MDM exploits have been found and systems have been compromised. A significant risk is shown in the following presentation that exploits badly configured PEAP on wi-fi networks: www.defcon.org/images /defcon-21/dc-21-presentations/Yavor/DEFCON-21-Yavor-The-BYOD-PEAP-Show-Updated.pdf.

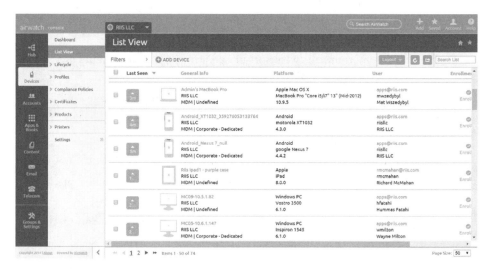

Figure 8-6   AirWatch MDM solution

Conclusion

With every version of Android there are multiple patches and changes that may have an effect on your security. We looked at the adb backup command as well as some commands for reading logs from other apps. But there are no doubt more. For example, it's reported that Android 4.1.1 is affected by the Heartbleed SSL issue (https://bluebox.com/technical/heartbleed-bug-impacts-mobile-devices). We also looked at how Android Encryption can be used to protect your device. Finally, we explained how SEAndroid and Samsung Knox fit into the security of your device.

Google has announced an agreement with Samsung to integrate the Knox components into Android L, so this is coming very soon to every non-Samsung Android user. This is a nice segue into the next chapter where we try to predict the future of Android security.

9

The Future

In this final chapter we take a look at some more sophisticated attacks on the Android platform. We also look at the Internet of Things (IoT) in the world of Android to see how that also might be vulnerable to attack and to get ideas about what we can do to stop these attacks. We look at outside influences, such as HIPAA and PCI compliance, that you'll need to understand, because before too long they are going to impact the Android security landscape. And, finally, we look at what's likely to come in the future from Google and other third-party companies to help you protect your apps.

More Sophisticated Attacks

As has been mentioned several times before in this book, the examples of insecure coding techniques that we've used come from real-world apps that we've encountered in a more or less ad hoc fashion over the past two to three years.

At its most basic, the insecure coding practices fall into the following categories:

- Usernames and passwords stored as cleartext in shared preferences
- Credit card data stored as cleartext in shared preferences
- Encryption keys hard coded in the APK, exposing passwords or credit card data
- Unencrypted network traffic
- API keys hard coded in the APK

These examples are not very sophisticated and yet are still very common. So if you don't store any information on the client, if you always use SSL correctly, and if you use asymmetric public/private key encryption, then you're going to be much more secure than your peers. But the Android platform is still relatively new—there will be more sophisticated attacks coming.

Let's look at something a bit more difficult to address than someone backing up your data or decompiling your APK. In this example we'll show how someone might want to hijack an Android Intent if you're using an implicit rather than an explicit Intent.

The Android framework allows apps and components within apps to communicate with one another by passing messages, called Intents. These Intents are essentially an API for one app to invoke another via messaging, and they can be either implicit or explicit. We'll show exactly what that means in the following example.

The example shows a simple Login app that takes a username, password, and email address and passes that to an IntentReceiverActivity to check the credentials against a database, for example.

So let's take a look at how someone might hijack an Intent.

Here we're using a simple login page, which has a username, password, and email address, and it's calling an Intent implicitly to handle the login information.

The application is pretty simple. Enter your username, password, and email address in the Login Screen and the IntentReceiverActivity picks it up and displays it on the page (see Figure 9-1).

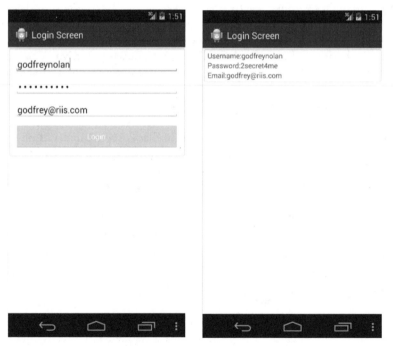

Figure 9-1   LoginIntent app

Listing 9-1 shows the code for the Login screen.

Listing 9-1 **Login App**

```
package com.riis.login;

import android.os.Bundle;
import android.app.Activity;
import android.content.Intent;
import android.view.View;
import android.widget.Button;
import android.widget.EditText;

public class LoginActivity extends Activity {

  Button loginButton;
  EditText usernameField, passwordField, emailField;


    @Override
    protected void onCreate(Bundle savedInstanceState) {
        super.onCreate(savedInstanceState);
        setContentView(R.layout.login _ screen);

        usernameField = (EditText) findViewById (R.id.username _ field);
        passwordField = (EditText) findViewById(R.id.password _ field);
        emailField = (EditText) findViewById(R.id.email _ field);
      loginButton = (Button) findViewById(R.id.login _ button);

        loginButton.setOnClickListener(new View.OnClickListener() {
            @Override
            public void onClick(View v) {
             onSubmit(v);
             }
        });

    }

    public void onSubmit(View v){

    // implicit intent
    Intent intent = new Intent();                                    // line 38

    Bundle bundle = new Bundle();

    bundle.putString("Username", usernameField.getText().toString());
    bundle.putString("Password", passwordField.getText().toString());
    bundle.putString("Email", emailField.getText().toString());

    intent.setAction("com.riis.login.IntentReceiverActivity");
```

```
        intent.addCategory(Intent.CATEGORY _ DEFAULT);
        intent.putExtras(bundle);

        startActivity(intent);


    }

}
```

At line 38 we see where the MainActivity hands off to the IntentReceiverActivity:

```
    // implicit
    Intent intent = new Intent();
```

Implicit Intents such as these leave it to the Android OS to manage the Intent communication. You or an attacker can find the Intents in the AndroidManifest.xml file as shown in Listing 9-2.

Listing 9-2   **AndroidManifest.xml**

```xml
<?xml version="1.0" encoding="utf-8"?>
<manifest xmlns:android="http://schemas.android.com/apk/res/android"
    package="com.riis.login"
    android:versionCode="1"
    android:versionName="1.0" >

    <uses-sdk
        android:minSdkVersion="8" />

    <application
        android:allowBackup="true"
        android:icon="@drawable/ic _ launcher"
        android:label="@string/app _ name"
        android:theme="@style/AppTheme" >
        <activity
            android:name="com.riis.login.LoginActivity"
            android:label="@string/app _ name" >
            <intent-filter>
                <action android:name="android.intent.action.MAIN" />
                <category android:name="android.intent.category.LAUNCHER" />
            </intent-filter>
        </activity>
        <activity
            android:name="com.riis.login.IntentReceiverActivity"
            android:label="@string/app _ name" >
            <intent-filter>
                <action android:name="com.riis.login.IntentReceiverActivity" />
                <category android:name="android.intent.category.DEFAULT" />
            </intent-filter>
        </activity>
    </application>

</manifest>
```

Android knows that it should pass the control to the `IntentReceiverActivity` given that it's the default category Intent as well as the only other Intent in the file:

```
<intent-filter>
        <action android:name="com.riis.login.IntentReceiverActivity" />
        <category android:name="android.intent.category.DEFAULT" />
</intent-filter>
```

So what if we listen in to Intent communication and hijack the communication? We can use apktool to look at what Intents your target app is using and then open up the AndroidManifest.xml file to see what Intents are there.

```
java -jar apktool.jar d Login.apk
```

With an implicit Intent we can try to hijack the code by telling Android that we want to receive the Intent in our AndroidManisfest.xml file. Listing 9-3 shows the HelloIntent AndroidManifest.xml file for the hijacked app.

Listing 9-3   **HelloIntent AndroidManifest.xml**

```
<?xml version="1.0" encoding="utf-8"?>
<manifest xmlns:android="http://schemas.android.com/apk/res/android"
    package="com.riis.hellointent"
    android:versionCode="1"
    android:versionName="1.0" >

    <uses-sdk
        android:minSdkVersion="8"
        android:targetSdkVersion="18" />

    <application
        android:allowBackup="true"
        android:icon="@drawable/ic _ launcher"
        android:label="@string/app _ name"
        android:theme="@style/AppTheme" >
        <activity
            android:name="com.riis.hellointent.MainActivity"
            android:label="@string/app _ name" >
            <intent-filter>
                <action android:name="android.intent.action.MAIN" />
                <category android:name="android.intent.category.LAUNCHER" />
            </intent-filter>
            <intent-filter>
                <action android:name="com.riis.login.IntentReceiverActivity" />
                <category android:name="android.intent.category.DEFAULT" />
            </intent-filter>
        </activity>
    </application>

</manifest>
```

The new receiver code (see Listing 9-4) captures the Login credentials and displays them in the form of a toast message.

Listing 9-4   **HelloIntent**

```java
package com.riis.hellointent;

import android.os.Bundle;
import android.app.Activity;
import android.view.Menu;
import android.widget.Toast;

public class MainActivity extends Activity {

    @Override
    protected void onCreate(Bundle savedInstanceState) {
        super.onCreate(savedInstanceState);
        setContentView(R.layout.activity_main);

        Toast.makeText(getBaseContext(), "username: " + this.getIntent().getString
        Extra("Username")+
                "\npassword: "+this.getIntent().getStringExtra("Password")+
                  "\nemail: "+this.getIntent().getStringExtra("Email"),
                Toast.LENGTH_LONG).show();

    }

}
```

Now when we run the Login we have a choice of receivers. If we choose the wrong receiver, the Intent is hijacked and username and password are captured by our little malware app. If we now make the Intent explicit and tell it to only use the IntentReceiverActivity, the Intent can no longer be hijacked (see Listing 9-5).

Listing 9-5   **Fixed LoginIntent code**

```java
package com.riis.login;

import android.os.Bundle;
import android.app.Activity;
import android.content.Intent;
import android.view.View;
import android.widget.Button;
import android.widget.EditText;

public class LoginActivity extends Activity {

    Button loginButton;
    EditText usernameField, passwordField, emailField;


    @Override
    protected void onCreate(Bundle savedInstanceState) {
```

```
        super.onCreate(savedInstanceState);
        setContentView(R.layout.login_screen);

        usernameField = (EditText) findViewById   (R.id.username_field);
        passwordField = (EditText) findViewById(R.id.password_field);
        emailField = (EditText) findViewById(R.id.email_field);
        loginButton = (Button) findViewById(R.id.login_button);

        loginButton.setOnClickListener(new View.OnClickListener() {
            @Override
            public void onClick(View v) {
                onSubmit(v);
            }
        });

    }

    public void onSubmit(View v){

        // implicit
        // Intent intent = new Intent();

        // explicit
        Intent intent = new Intent(this, IntentReceiverActivity.class);   // line 41

        Bundle bundle = new Bundle();

        bundle.putString("Username", usernameField.getText().toString());
        bundle.putString("Password", passwordField.getText().toString());
        bundle.putString("Email", emailField.getText().toString());

        intent.setAction("com.riis.login.IntentReceiverActivity");
        intent.addCategory(Intent.CATEGORY_DEFAULT);
        intent.putExtras(bundle);

        startActivity(intent);


    }

}
```

On line 41 we're now explicitly telling the app what Intent to use:

```
// explicit
Intent intent = new Intent(this, IntentReceiverActivity.class);   // line 41
```

The HelloIntent app no longer gets the Intent notification, so it can't hijack these apps.

You can also listen in to see what broadcast and Intent communication is happening using the Intent Sniffer, which you can download from isecpartners.com (see Figure 9-2). This is a great way to see what your app is exposing and what you need to look for beyond the exploits that we covered in earlier chapters.

Figure 9-2   Intent Sniffer

Internet of Things

The Android footprint is no longer limited to phones and tablets. It is embedded in lots of other devices, from TVs to watches to cars, and the list is only going to grow. There are also lots of other devices that interact with your existing Android devices that have to be secured.

Android Wearables

Google released the Android Wear SDK at Google I/O 2014. It allows developers to write Android apps for watches. At the time of this writing there are a small number of these devices currently available, such as the LG G watch and the Moto 360. While an Android Wear watch is tethered to your phone, it is still an independent Android device running on a Linux kernel.

Just like a phone, you can turn on the developer options on an Android watch and enable debugging (see Figure 9-3), and then shell onto the device using the adb shell

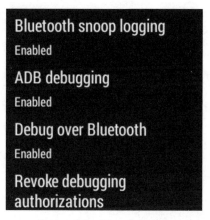

Figure 9-3   Google watch

command. The directory structure is similar to a phone or tablet, with the apps in the /data/app folder and the user data in /data/data. It is different from a phone or tablet in a number of ways though. Android Wear devices are not customizable by the OEMS and auto update to the latest OS, which enables security patches to automatically appear on your watch much more quickly than on phones.

A watch is more likely to be lost or dumped on eBay than a phone, so make sure there is no personal information stored on the watch that you would not want someone to access if someone finds or buys the watch secondhand. These devices are no doubt going to have a wide range of fitness apps. The Moto 360 comes with a heart rate monitor and Android Wear devices can already be rooted (see http://blog.laptopmag.com/root-lg-g-watch). So if you're writing something for the Android Wear device, make sure that little or no information is stored on it.

Ford Sync AppID

At the time of this writing the Android Auto SDK has not been released, but there are still a number of different ways to get your Android phone to talk to your car. The Ford Sync API works on a number of Ford cars that have the correct version of Sync. It allows the Ford voice-operated dashboard to act like a remote control for your app.

Converting an app consists of mapping the Sync buttons to the events on your app. It also involves applying for an AppID from Ford; they have to approve your app before they'll send you an AppID.

Listing 9-6 shows how to start the Ford Sync proxy with an AppID. Your app will not be able to talk to Ford Sync cars without having an approved AppID, so it's important to keep it safe. Hard coding the AppID in the Java source means that it could be used by someone else, someone who decompiles the code and then uses it to talk to the Ford Sync without authorization. Getting a new AppID may be difficult if it does get compromised; the "Key Management" section in Chapter 4 can help you keep the AppID safer.

Listing 9-6   **AppID**

```
public void startProxy() {
        if (proxy == null) {
            try {
                proxy = new SyncProxyALM(this,"Better Driving",true,"1647813557");
            } catch (SyncException e) {
                e.printStackTrace();
                //error creating proxy, returned proxy = null
                if (proxy == null){
                    stopSelf();
                }
            }
        }
    }
```

Audits and Compliance

To date there hasn't been much in the way of the industry converging on a set of mobile security compliance standards that developers have to follow. The PCI guidelines are not mandatory—they are still just guidelines. The HIPAA requirements that we covered in Chapter 1 are not written for mobile security—it would be safe to say that they were written for a different era, where medical software amounted to client/server applications running on desktop PCs locked in a medical office. But even though HIPAA has not caught up the technology they still apply to smartphones, which in many cases have no physical barriers to accessing an end user's device.

We looked at the HIPAA technical requirements at the beginning of this book. Some of these requirements are not common in mobile development. Take the following three requirements:

> Does your practice retain copies of its audit/access records?

> Does your practice have audit control mechanisms that can monitor, record, and/ or examine information system activity?

> Does your practice analyze the activities performed by all of its workforce and service providers to identify the extent to which each needs access to ePHI?

These requirements are attempting to safeguard the end user to make sure only the proper authorized users are accessing the electronic protected health information (ePHI). It should be irrelevant if someone can decompile or disassemble your code.

And if it does reveal something that you don't want to expose, such as an encryption key, then it's not HIPAA secure.

One of the recommendations in this book is to not only log access on the server, but in order to be HIPAA compliant, every page and detail accessed needs to be logged on the server and tools need to be put in place so that a single user's access can be monitored in real time and recorded for access after a break-in.

If mobile applications today are collecting any of this information, then it's probably being used for analytics and marketing purposes rather than for HIPAA compliance. As the medical market for apps matures, expect to have to do a lot more auditing of your users for these compliance reasons. Offline logging will also have to be encrypted, which as we've seen can be very problematic.

Even though it is very difficult to make sure your app is HIPAA secure and that you are in compliance, there are some excellent resources to help you. The Healthcare Information and Management Systems Society (HIMMS) has released a very good mobile health roadmap, which you can find at www.himss.org/mobilehealthit/roadmap. And while it covers all mobile devices, not just smartphones, it is an excellent resource for navigating the regulatory framework, from BYOD in a medical setting to recommendations on best practices for securing your app. Those best practices, which originally came from the Department of Homeland Security, follow:

- Purchase only those networkable medical devices that have well-documented and fine-grained security features available, and be sure that the medical IT network engineers can configure safely on their networks.

- Include in purchasing vehicles vendor support for ongoing firmware, patch, and antivirus updates where they are a suitable risk mitigation strategy. Operate well-maintained external-facing firewalls, network monitoring techniques, intrusion detection techniques, and internal network segmentation containing the medical devices, to the extent practical.

- Configure access control lists (ACL) on these network segments so that only positively authorized accounts can access them.

- Establish strict policies for the connection of any networked devices, particularly wireless devices, to the Health Information Network (HIN), including laptops, tablets, USB devices, PDAs, smartphones, and so forth, such that no access to networked resources is provided to unsecured and/or unrecognized devices.

- Establish policies to maintain, review, and audit network configurations as routine activities when the medical IT network is changed.

- Use the principle of least privilege to decide which accounts need access to specific medical device segments, rather than providing access to the whole network.

- Implement safe and effective, but legal, patch and software upgrade policies for medical IT networks, which contain regulated medical devices.

- Secure communication channels, particularly wireless ones, through the use of encryption and authentication at both ends of a communication channel.

- Have and enforce password policies to protect patient information.

Tools

Virtual machines like the Dalvik Virtual Machine (DVM) have been around for almost as long as computing. We have several early examples, such as the Java Virtual Machine (JVM) and Microsoft's Common Language Runtime (CLR), which we can look at to see what happened in the past that might help us predict the future for the Android framework.

Java decompilers, such as Mocha and Jad, appeared relatively quickly in the early days of Java, and there was a small rush of commercial and open source Java obfuscators and source code protection tools that were written to combat these tools. For a while the decompilers and obfuscators were in a race to write code that would stop the decompilers from working, and then a new release of the decompiler would appear that would combat this attack. We have seen something similar already, where DexGuard inserts code that prevents dex2jar from working.

The biggest change in the near future is that the tools that decompile and obfuscate are going to move away from working on Java opcodes and toward Android or Dalvik opcodes. Decompiling an Android app has been a two-stage process to date: dex2jar converts the classes.dex to java jar files and then JD-GUI decompiles the Java classes. ProGuard, DashO, and others obfuscate the java jar files before they are converted to classes.dex. There really is no reason why tools couldn't just work on the classes.dex files. Jadx, the Android decompiler, already does this, so expect more classes.dex decompilers and obfuscators to follow. Expect to see third-party libraries post-process your APK. These will unpack your APK, instrument your classes.dex file, and apply the necessary changes to add analytics or defect tracking. This lack of visibility makes it even more important to *trust but verify* any code added to your APK.

Google is already moving away from the DVM, which will be replaced by a new virtual machine, the Android Runtime (ART). So far ART uses the same opcodes as the DVM, but now they are optimized ahead of time for better performance rather than any improvements in source code protection. Google will also continue to increase the security of its devices using SEAndroid and a version of KNOX.

There are significant changes coming in the devices themselves. At the time of printing, Android L is due to be released, which should have device encryption turned on by default. And if it's not in Android L, it will probably be in the version after Android L. A much cheaper phone, Android One, has been released, which will dramatically increase Android's reach. Android Silver has also been announced, which is a standard Android image for OEM's moving forward, which Google hopes will provide consistency across models and help with fragmentation. Android Studio will also be the only real choice of IDE for developing Android apps.

Drozer

If the past is any help with our predictions, developing in Android will become more complex with more APIs and more frameworks gradually introduced, similar to the way the complexity of Java and .Net has grown in the past decade.

As part of your process, it makes sense to use a tool that has the latest exploits baked in to help with penetration testing of your apps. One such tool is Drozer from MWR, which is available at https://www.mwrinfosecurity.com/products/drozer/.

To run a test Drozer, take the following steps:

1. Download and install Drozer.

2. Install the Drozer agent on your emulator or device that comes with the download:

   ```
   adb install agent.apk.
   ```

3. Use port forwarding to connect to the agent, as in the following command:

   ```
   adb forward tcp:31415 tcp:31415
   ```

4. Start the agent and turn on the embedded server (see Figure 9-4).

5. Run the command drozer console connect and you should get the dz> prompt.

MWR provides a test APK to help you learn how to use Drozer. You can download it from http://mwr.to/sieve and then use adb install sieve.apk to push it to your device.

Drozer has a number of attacks that you can run to test the apk. For example, the following command sees which activities are exported by Sieve:

```
dz> run app.package.attacksurface com.mwr.example.sieve
Attack Surface:
  3 activities exported
  0 broadcast receivers exported
  2 content providers exported
  2 services exported
    is debuggable
dz>
```

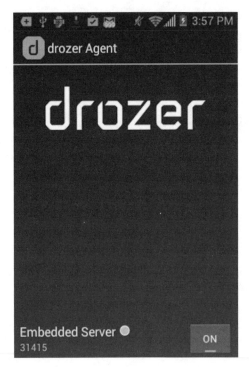

Figure 9-4   Drozer agent

This tells us that there are three activities and two services that are potentially open to attack. The APK is also debuggable, which shouldn't happen, so we can attach to the APK in debug mode.

Next we can view the list of exported Activities using the app.activity.info command:

```
dz> run app.activity.info -f com.mwr.example.sieve
Package: com.mwr.example.sieve
 com.mwr.example.sieve.FileSelectActivity
 com.mwr.example.sieve.MainLoginActivity
 com.mwr.example.sieve.PWList
dz>
```

From the list of these three activities, PWList looks the most interesting. Using the app.activity.start command from the Drozer command line we can launch the Activity directly, completely bypassing the login screens:

```
dz> run app.activity.start --component com.mwr.example.sieve com.mwr.example.
sieve.PWList
dz>
```

Drozer is a great example of an Android pen testing tool that provides a single interface which allows you to attack an APK's activities, database, files, and content providers in a consistent, repeatable manner.

OWASP Mobile Top 10 Risks

This book and the LiveLesson video are based on the OWASP Top 10 Mobile Risks. There are a number of people watching the latest developments, and from time to time the OWASP Top 10 Mobile Risks change. In fact, it's already changed in the last 12 months. Keep an eye on future risks as they appear at https://www.owasp.org /index.php/OWASP_Mobile_Security_Project#tab=Top_10_Mobile_Risks.

Like MWRInfoSecurity, OWASP also provides some sample apps to help increase your understanding of the different attacks that someone can perform on your APK. These are GoatDroid and Herd Financial, which are examples of a social app and a financial app.

Lint

Many of the current security issues can be found using Lint and looking at any warnings flagged in the security category (see Figure 9-5). In this case it shows that we haven't set the `android:allowBackup` to false in the AndroidManifest.xml file.

Google will continue to add Security issues to the Lint Security Category sooner or later. They are already addressing more sophisticated attacks, not just the simple mistakes such as making a file MODE_WORLD_READABLE.

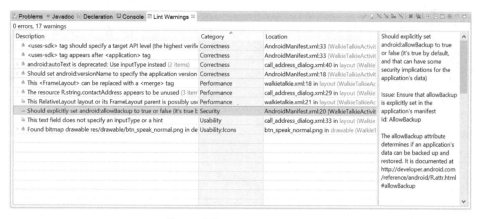

Figure 9-5   Lint security tags

Conclusion

In this chapter we've done our best to point in the direction of where hackers are going to attack your code. As developers raise their game and fix the simple things, such as not exposing usernames and passwords or credit card information, the level of attacks will get more sophisticated. We looked at the Internet of Things and how the extended Android footprint also needs to be protected. Finally, we've attempted to predict the future of Android security, and we've looked at how future attacks and defense will likely move to Android's classes.dex and away from Java jar files.

Index

Numbers

010 hex editor, xviii

37signals, OAuth support, 77

A

Abe (Android Backup Extractor), xviii

Access control

    authentication best practices, 54–55

    function-level, 147

    gaining superuser access, 102–103

Access control lists (ACLs), HIMMS guidelines, 189

Accessory devices

    Ford Sync API, 187–188

    wearables, 186–187

Accountability, OWASP Cloud top 10 risks, 148

ACLs (access control lists), HIMMS guidelines, 189

adb command

    backing up Android database, 111–114

    backing up Android devices, 169

    decompiling APK, 4

    description of, xviii

AdMob hack, Pandora and, 152–154

AES symmetric key algorithm, 92–93

Ahead-Of-Time (AOT) compilers, 7

Air Watch MDM solution, from VMware, 177–178

allowBackup attribute, disabling backup functionality, 115–116

Android application package. See APK (Android application package)

Android apps. See Apps

Android Backup Extractor (Abe), xviii

Android HelloWorld app, 39–41

Android OSs

adb backup introduced in Ice Cream Sandwich, 169

    Android L release, 190

    ART (Android Runtime) and, 7

    cross-platform apps and, 135

    device security and, 167

    encryption functionality, 116

    encryption to be default in Android L, 173

    fragmentation and, 168

    Google App Encryption in Jelly Bean, 65

    Linux and, 17

    rooting the phone to test security of data transmission, 102

    SEAndroid security policies and, 174–175

Android L, 173, 178, 190

Android Runtime (ART)

    overview of, 7

    replacing DVM, 190

Android Silver, 191

Android Studio, 191

AndroidID, supplementing authentication process, 59–62

AntiLVL test suite

    example code, 68–74

    for removing license checking, 68

AOT (Ahead-Of-Time) compilers, 7

API keys

asymmetric encryption of, 94–99

insecure coding practices, 179

protecting, 88–92, 131

replay attacks and, 135

symmetric encryption of, 92–94

APK (Android application package)

comparing Android security with iOS, 1–2

decompiling, 4–6, 28–29

disassembly, 43–45

pulling off devices, 119

reasons for adding third-party libraries, 151

reassembly, 45–48

third-parties libraries and, 190

apktool

description of, xviii

reassembly of APK, 45–48

AppID

Ford Sync AppID, 187–188

using as encryption key for Android database, 127

Application licenses. *See* **Licenses, application**

Apps

adding LVL to, 65–66

adding SQLite database to, 111–114

Android HelloWorld app, 39–41

cross-platform. *See* Cross-platform apps

finding package name of, 114

hybrid. *See* Hybrid apps

installing Crashlytics app, 157–159

installing Critercism app, 154–156

mobile. *See* Mobile apps

protecting in Google Play, 65

risk of third-party libraries and, 152

session management, 82–84

Smali HelloWorld app, 41–43

testing logins on, 85

ART (Android Runtime)

overview of, 7

replacing DVM, 190

Assembly/disassembly

Android HelloWorld app, 39–41

disassembly example (remove app store check), 43–48

Smali and Baksmali for classes.dex files, 39

Smali HelloWorld app, 41–43

Asymmetric keys. *See also* **Encryption**

compared with symmetric, 92

securing network communications, 94–99

Attacks/hacks

hacking mobile apps and websites, 131

hacking usernames and passwords, 53

increasing sophistication of, 179–186

man-in-the-middle. *See* MITM (man-in-the-middle) attacks

replay attacks, 135

SQL injection. *See* SQL injection attacks

WebView. *See* WebView attacks

Audits, 188–190

Authentication

adding licensing verification library, 65–66

AntiLVL test suite, 68–74

applying licensing verification library, 66

best practices, 54–55

decompiling LVL code, 75–77

encrypting passwords, 62–65

examples, 55–65

Google licensing guidelines, 66–68

licensing applications, 65

managing web and mobile sessions, 82–84

OAuth and, 77–78

OAuth use with Facebook, 78–82

OWASP guidelines, 15, 133, 146

securing logins, 51–54

supplementing authentication process with AndroidID, 59–62

two (or more) factor authentication, 85

usernames and passwords and, 84–85

validating email, 57–58

Authorization, OWASP guidelines, 15, 133

Availability, OWASP guidelines, 132

AXMLPrinter2, xviii

B

BAA (Business Associate Agreement), 150

Backing up Android database

adb for, 111–114

disabling backup functionality, 115–116

Backing up Android devices, 169

Baksmali

assembly/disassembly of classes.dex files, 39

description of, xix

Binary code, OWASP guidelines, 16

Bring Your Own Device (BYOD), 177

Build process, 3

Burp Suite, SQL injection attack with, 142–144

Business Associate Agreement (BAA), 150

Business continuity, OWASP Cloud top 10 risks, 148

Business needs, Forrester Research top 10 security issues, 16

Business rules, hiding, 48–49

BYOD (Bring Your Own Device), 177

Bytecode, obfuscation of, 38

C

C++

disassembly, 48–49

hiding encryption keys in C++, 124–127

Calabash, testing logins, 85

CAs (Certificate Authorities)

encryption providers, 87

server authentication, 133

SSL certifications from, 99–100, 104

Charles Proxy

description of, xix

generating SSL certificates with, 99

MITM (man-in-the-middle) attacks on third-party apps, 163

testing security of network traffic, 103–107

viewing network traffic with, 91–92

Classes.dex

converting into jar files, 6

converting into Java .class format, 5

file structure, 19–23

securing Android in future and, 190

Clients

authentication best practices, 54

OWASP client-side security guidelines, 15

Closure tool, for obfuscation of code in cross-platform app, 139–140

Cloud, OWASP risks, 146–149

CLR (Common Language Runtime), 190

Code protection

Android HelloWorld app, 39–41

classes.dex file structure, 19–23

DexGuard obfuscator, 32–37

disassembly example (remove app store check), 43–48

hiding business rules in NDK, 48–49

obfuscation best practices, 24–25

ProGuard obfuscator, 27–32

security through obscurity, 38

Smali HelloWorld app, 41–43

taxonomy of obfuscation, 34

testing and obfuscation, 38–39

viewing APK without obfuscation, 26–27

Colberg, Christian, 32

Common Language Runtime (CLR), 190

Communication security

HIMMS guidelines, 190

networking and. *See* Network communication security

Compilers/decompilers

AOT (Ahead-Of-Time) compilers, 7

converting VM code back to source code, 2

decompiled code without obfuscation, 26–27

decompiling APK, 4–6

decompiling LVL code, 75–77

decompiling SDK's, 160–163

DexGuard decompiler, 35

ProGuard decompiler, 28–29

securing Android in future and, 190

Compliance. *See* Regulatory compliance

Component vulnerability, OWASP Top 10 risks, 147

Confidentiality, OWASP Web Services Cheat Sheet, 133

Configuration files, ProGuard, 27

Crashlytics app, installing, 157–159

credentials.xml file, 52

Critercism app, 154–156

Cross-platform apps

Closure for obfuscation of code, 139–140

commenting code, 135–137

JavaScript compressors for obfuscation of code, 137–139

overview of, 135

Cross-site request forgery (CSRF), 147

Cross-Site Scripting. *See* XSS (Cross-Site Scripting)

Cryptography. *See also* Encryption

Android libraries, 87

FIPS 140-2 standard, 176–177

OWASP guidelines, 15

CSRF (cross-site request forgery), 147

Cucumber, login testing with, 85

Cydia Impactor, gaining superuser access, 102–103

D

DAC (Discretionary Access Control), 174

Dalvik Debug Monitor Server (DDMS), 169

Dalvik Virtual Machine. *See* DVM (Dalvik Virtual Machine)

DashO

obfuscation with, 34

securing Android in future and, 190

Data

leakage and storage, 15

OWASP Cloud top 10 risks, 148–149

sensitive. *See* Sensitive data

Databases

backing using adb, 111–114

disabling backup, 115–116

encrypting data using SQLCipher, 116–118

finding the encryption key, 119

hiding encryption keys by using device-specific keys, 123–124

hiding encryption keys in C++ using NDK, 124–127

hiding encryption keys in shared preferences, 122–123

hiding encryption keys using web services, 127

overview of, 109

requiring encryption key be used for each access, 120–121

security issues, 109–110

SQL injection attacks and, 127–129

SQLite and, 110–111

DDMS (Dalvik Debug Monitor Server), 169

Debugging, logs and, 169–172

Decompilers. *See* Compilers/decompilers

Dedexer, xix

Defect tracking apps

installing Crashlytics app, 157–159

installing Critercism app, 154–156

Design, Forrester Research top 10 security issues, 17

Developers/development, Forrester Research top 10 security issues, 16–17

Device ID

authentication, 51–53

protecting apps in Google Play, 65

Device security

backing up with adb, 169

encryption, 172–174

FIPS 140-2 standard, 18, 176–177

fragmentation and, 168

HIMMS guidelines, 189

logs, 169–172

MDM (Mobile Device Management), 177–178

overview of, 17, 167–168

SEAndroid for identifying security gaps, 174–175

wiping devices, 168

Device-specific keys, hiding encryption keys, 123–124

Dex files, 2. See also Classes.dex

dex2jar tool

changing Android bytecode into Java bytecode, 22

converting classes.dex into jar files, 6

converting dex files into Java .class format, 5

description of, xix

securing Android in future and, 190

DexGuard

code protection, 35–37

description of, xix

enabling, 34–35

securing Android in future and, 190

Disassemblers. See Assembly/disassembly

Discretionary Access Control (DAC), 174

Dropbox, OAuth support, 77

Drozer

description of, xix

penetration testing with, 191–193

DVM (Dalvik Virtual Machine)

Android running on, 1

JIT (Just in Time) compiler in, 7

securing Android in future and, 190

Smali files as ASCII representation of Dalvik opcodes, 39

dx command, converting jar files into dex files, 2

E

Education lacking, Forrester Research top 10 security issues, 16

electronic protected health information (ePHI), 188

Email

authentication best practices, 54

authentication examples, 55–56

validating email addresses, 57–58

Encryption

to be default in Android L, 173

device security, 172–174

FIPS 140-2 standard, 176–177

generating encryption key, 62–63

Google App Encryption, 65

HIPAA compliance, 189

insecure coding practices, 179

message integrity and confidentiality, 133

of network communication using asymmetric keys, 94–99

of network communication using symmetric keys, 92–94

OWASP Cloud top 10 risks, 149

of passwords, 63–65

preventing replay attacks, 135

for sensitive data, 55

wiping devices and, 168

Encryption, of Android database

finding the encryption key, 119

hiding encryption keys by using device-specific keys, 123–124

hiding encryption keys in NDK, 124–127

Encryption, of Android database (*Continued*)

hiding encryption keys in shared preferences, 122–123

hiding encryption keys using web services, 127

requiring encryption key be used for each access, 120–121

using SQLCipher, 116–118

ePHI (electronic protected health information), 188

F

Facebook

data security and, xv

OAuth support, 77

Factory reset, wiping devices, 168

Federal Information Processing Standard (FIPS) 140-2 device standard, 18, 176–177

FIPS (Federal Information Processing Standard) 140-2 standard, 18, 176–177

Firesheep app, 99

Ford Sync AppID, 187–188

Forrester Research, top 10 nontechnical mobile security risks, 16–17

Forwarding, handling unvalidated redirects, 147

Fragmentation, device security and, 168

G

GitHub, OAuth support, 77

GoDaddy, sources of SSL certs, 104

Google

App Encryption, 65

licensing guidelines, 66–68

protecting apps in Google Play, 65

Security Best Practices, 9–10

Guidelines, security

Forrester Research's top 10 nontechnical mobile security risks, 16–17

Google Security Best Practices, 9–10

overview of, 7

OWASP Top 10 mobile risks, 14–16

PCI Mobile Payment Acceptance Security Guidelines, 7–8

Security Risk Assessment Tool for testing HIPAA compliance, 10–14

H

Hardware, fragmentation and, 168

Health Information Network (HIN), 189

Health Insurance Portability and Accountability Act. *See* HIPAA (Health Insurance Portability and Accountability Act)

Healthcare Information and Management Systems Society (HIMMS), 189–190

HealthIT.gov, Security Risk Assessment Tool, 10

HelloWorld apps

Android, 39–41

Smali, 41–43

HIMMS (Healthcare Information and Management Systems Society), 189–190

HIN (Health Information Network), 189

HIPAA (Health Insurance Portability and Accountability Act)

device security and, 167

encryption of sensitive data required in, 173

regulatory compliance, 148

requirements, 188–190

Security Risk Assessment Tool for, 10–14

sensitive data and, 88

third-parties libraries and, 152

unencrypted data in SQLite database not compliant with, 111

web server compliance, 149–150

HTTP/HTTPS

connecting using API keys, 88

connection security and, 87

effectiveness of SSL and, 99

example calls to Weather Underground, 88–91

testing security of network traffic with Charles Proxy, 103–107

testing SSL security with man-in-the-middle attack, 100–102

testing third-party apps with man-in-the-middle attacks, 163

viewing network traffic with Charles Proxy, 91–92

Human factors, Forrester Research top 10 security issues, 16

Hybrid apps

cross-platform apps compared with, 140

securing, 131

I

Ice Cream Sandwich (Android 4.0), 102, 173

IDA Pro, hexadecimal editor, 48–49

Incidence analysis, 149

Information Technology Management Reform Act (1996), 18

Infrastructure security, 149

Insecure Direct Object References, OWASP Top 10 risks, 146

Intent sniffer, 186

Intents, hijacking Android Intent, 180–185

Internet of Things (IoT)

Ford Sync AppID, 187–188

wearables, 186–187

iOS

binary code and, 1

comparing Android security with, 1–2

cross-platform apps and, 135

Objective-C code and, 49

PCI Mobile Payment Acceptance Security Guidelines and, 7

IoT (Internet of Things)

Ford Sync AppID, 187–188

wearables, 186–187

J

Jadx, xix

jar files

adding third-party libraries to APK, 151

converting classes.dex files into, 6

converting into dex files, 2

Java decompilers, 2

Java Virtual Machine (JVM), 190

JavaScript compressors, for obfuscation of code in cross-platform app, 137–139

JD-GUI

decompiling SDK of third-party library, 160–163

description of, xix

pulling APK off devices, 119

securing Android in future and, 190

Jelly Bean (Android 4.1), 169. *See also* **Android OSs**

JIT (Just in Time) compiler, in DVM, 7

Just in Time (JIT) compiler, in DVM, 7

JVM (Java Virtual Machine), 190

K

Keyczar

description of, xix

getting asymmetric key from, 95

Keys, encryption

asymmetric keys, 94–99

encrypting sensitive data, 55

message integrity and, 133

symmetric keys, 92–94

KitKat. *See also* **Android OSs**

ART (Android Runtime) and, 7

fragmentation and, 168

SEAndroid and, 17, 174–175

L

Least privilege principle, HIMMS guidelines, 189

Libraries

cryptography, 87, 176

licensing verification. *See* LVL (licensing verification library)

PHP Nonce Library, 135

third-party. *See* Third-parties libraries

Licenses, application

adding licensing verification library to apps, 65–66

AntiLVL test suite, 68–74

applying licensing verification library, 66

decompiling LVL code, 75–77

Google licensing guidelines, 66–68

overview of, 65

licensing verification library. *See* LVL (licensing verification library)

Lint

description of, xix

tagging security issues, 193

LogCat, filtering logs with, 169

Logins

hijacking Android Intent, 180–185

OWASP login session guidelines, 15

policies, 56–57

securing, 51–54

SQL injection attacks and, 128–129

testing on Android apps, 85

using login password to encrypt Android database, 120–121

Logs, device security and, 169–172

LVL (licensing verification library)

adding to apps, 65–66

AntiLVL test suite, 68–74

applying, 66

decompiling LVL code, 75–77

Google licensing guidelines, 66–68

M

MAC (Mandatory Access Control), 174–175

Man-in-the-middle attacks. *See* MITM (man-in-the-middle) attacks

mapping.txt file, ProGuard, 29–31

MDM (Mobile Device Management), 177–178

Message integrity, OWASP Web Services Cheat Sheet, 133

Middleware Mandatory Access Control (MMAC), 175

MITM (man-in-the-middle) attacks

preventing, 133

rooting the phone and, 102–103

testing security of network traffic with Charles Proxy, 103–107

testing SSL security, 100–102

third-parties libraries and, 163

MMAC (Middleware Mandatory Access Control), 175

Mobile apps. *See also* Apps

data security and, xv

hacking, 131

HIPAA compliance, 189

session management, 82–84

WebView attacks, 140–142

Mobile Device Management (MDM), 177–178

Moto 360, wearables, 187

N

National Institute of Standards and Technology (NIST), 18

NDK (Native Developer Kit)

hiding business rules in, 48–49

hiding encryption keys in C++, 124–127

Network communication security

encryption using asymmetric keys, 94–99

encryption using symmetric keys, 92–94

HTTP/HTTPS connections and, 88–92

overview of, 87–88

rooting the phone to test security of data transmission, 102–103

SSL and, 99–100

testing security of network traffic with Charles Proxy, 103–107

testing SSL by performing man-in-the-middle attack, 100–102

NIST (National Institute of Standards and Technology), **18**

Nonce, preventing replay attacks, **135**

O

OAuth

handling unvalidated redirects, 147

overview of, 77–78

session management, 82–84

used with Facebook, 78–82

Obfuscation

best practices, 24–25

in cross-platform app, 137–140

decompiled code without obfuscation, 26–27

DexGuard obfuscator, 34–37

effectiveness of obfuscators, 38

ProGuard obfuscator, 27–32

securing Android in future and, 190

taxonomy of, 33–34

testing and, 38–39

Obfuscators

Google licensing guidelines and, 66

types of, 24

Open Web Application Security Project. *See* **OWASP (Open Web Application Security Project)**

OpenSSL FIPS library, cryptographic libraries, 176

OSs (operating system). *See* **Android OSs**

OTA (Over the Air) updates, 168

OWASP (Open Web Application Security Project)

Cloud top 10 risks, 148–149

mobile top 10 risks, 14–16, 193

Web Services Cheat Sheet, 133–134

web services top 10 risks, 146–147

P

Pandora, AdMob hack and, 152–154

Passwords

authentication examples, 55–56

best practices, 54

encrypting, 63–65

hacking, 53

hiding encryption keys in C++ using NDK, 124–127

HIMMS guidelines, 190

insecure coding practices, 179

protecting Android database, 120–121

securing logins, 51

sending over SSL, 99

storing in shared preferences file, 122–123

user behavior and, 84–85

PCI Mobile Payment Acceptance Security Guidelines, 7-8, 188

Penetration testing

with Drozer, 191–193

testing security configuration, 147

Permissions

least privilege principle, 189

third-parties libraries and, 152–154

trust but verify approach to third-party apps, 160

PHI (protected health information)

checking security of sensive data, 111

encryption required in HIPAA, 173

ePHI (electronic protected health information), 188

security of, 10, 14

third-parties libraries and, 152

PHP Nonce Library, 135

Physical security, OWASP Cloud top 10 risks, 149

Policies, HIMMS guidelines, 189-190

Privacy

Forrester Research top 10 security issues, 17

regulatory compliance, 148

Private keys. *See also* **Encryption**

in asymmetric encryption, 92

encrypting sensitive data, 55

message integrity and, 133

ProGuard

classes.dex file structure, 19–23

decompiling APK, 28–29

description of, xix

effectiveness of obfuscators, 38

enabling, 27–28

example of decompiled GUI, 32

files used by, 31

limitations of, 34

logs and, 170, 172

mapping.txt file, 29–31

obfuscation best practices, 24–27

obfuscation taxonomy, 33–34

overview of, 19

securing Android in future and, 190

testing and obfuscation, 38–39

Protected health information. *See* **PHI (protected health information)**

Proxy server, testing SSL security by performing man-in-the-middle attack, 100–102

Public keys

in asymmetric encryption, 92

encrypting sensitive data, 55

message integrity and, 133

Public Law 104-106, Information Technology Management Reform Act, 18

Q

QA (quality assurance), Forrester Research top 10 security issues, 17

R

Redirects, handling unvalidated, 147

Regulatory compliance

HIPAA requirements, 188–190

overview of, 148

OWASP Cloud top 10 risks, 148

Security Risk Assessment Tool for testing HIPAA compliance, 10–14

third-parties libraries and, 152

web servers and, 149–150

Replay attacks, 135

Resources inadequacy, Forrester Research top 10 security issues, 16

RESTful

OWASP Web Services Cheat Sheet, 132

web services, 132

Root the phone, to test security of data transmission, 102–103

S

SAML (Security Assertion Markup Language), 148

SDKs (software development kits)

Android Wear SDK, 186–187

decompiling SDK of third-party library, 160–163

MITM (man-in-the-middle) attacks on third-party SDKs, 163

SE (Security Enhanced) Android

for identifying device security gaps, 174–175

overview of, 17

securing Android in future and, 190

SE (Security Enhanced) Linux, 17, 174–175

Security

ART (Android Runtime) and, 7

benefits of Android, 1–2

code protection, 19

databases and, 109–110

decompiling an APK, 4–6

of devices. *See* Device security

FIPS (Federal Information Processing Standard), 18

Forrester Research's top 10 nontechnical mobile security risks, 16–17

Google Security Best Practices, 9–10

of network communication. *See* Network communication security

OWASP Top 10 mobile risks, 14–16

PCI Mobile Payment Acceptance Security Guidelines, 7–8

SE (Security Enhanced) Android, 17

security lists (guidelines), 7

Security Risk Assessment Tool for testing HIPAA compliance, 10–14

Security Assertion Markup Language (SAML), 148

Security Enhanced (SE) Android. *See* **SE (Security Enhanced) Android**

Security Enhanced (SE) Linux, 17, 174–175

Security Requirements for Cryptographic Modules Standard, 176

Security Risk Assessment (SRA) Tool, for testing HIPAA compliance, 10–14

Sensitive data. *See also* **PHI (protected health information)**

checking security of, 111

defined, 87–88

encrypting, 55, 116–118

OWASP Top 10 risks, 147

security issues with Android databases, 109–110

Servers

authentication best practices, 54

HIPAA compliance, 149–150

weak server-side control, 14–15

web services. *See* Web services

Session management

OWASP Top 10 risks, 146

web and mobile apps, 82–84

Session tokens, sending over SSL, 99

Shared preferences

hiding encryption keys, 122–123

insecure coding practices, 179

SQLite, 110

Smali

for assembly/disassembly of classes.dex files, 39

description of, xix

disassembly of APK into, 43–45

HelloWorld app, 41–43

SOAP

OWASP Web Services Cheat Sheet, 133

web services, 132

Software, fragmentation and, 168

Software development kits. *See* **SDKs (software development kits)**

SOX, regulatory compliance, 148

SQL injection attacks

Android databases and, 127–129

OWASP guidelines, 15

OWASP Top 10 risks, 146

WebView attacks, 142–144

SQLCipher

encrypting Android databases, 116–118

finding the SQLite encryption key, 119

hiding encryption keys by using device-specific keys, 123–124

loading encryption keys from resource folder, 122–123

viewing SQLite encryption keys, 119

SQLite

adding SQLCipher, 116–118

backing database using adb, 111–114

disabling backup, 115–116

overview of, 110–111

SQL injection attacks, 127–129

use for Android databases, 109

sqlitebrowser

description of, xix

viewing SQLite databases, 110–111

SRA (Security Risk Assessment) Tool, for testing HIPAA compliance, 10–14

SSL

overview of, 99–100

preventing man-in-the-middle attack, 133

rooting the phone to test security of data transmission, 102–103

testing SSL by performing man-in-the-middle attack, 100–102

Superuser access, gaining, 102–103

Symmetric keys. *See also* **Encryption**

asymmetric keys compared with, 94

encryption/decryption example, 93–94

Symmetric keys (*Continued*)

securing network communications, 92–93

T

Third-parties libraries

APK (Android application package) and, 190

decompiling SDK's, 160–163

installing, 154

installing Crashlytics app, 157–159

installing Critercism app, 154–156

MITM (man-in-the-middle) attacks and, 163

overview of, 151–152

permissions and, 152–154

transferring risks, 152

trusting and verifying, 160

Tokens

sending session tokens over SSL, 99

in session management, 82–84

Tools

in future of Android, 190–191

list of commonly used, xviii–xix

Transformations, security through obscurity, 38

Transport layer, OWASP guidelines, 15

Trust

SQL injection attacks, 15

trust but verify approach, 160

Two (or more) factor authentication, 54, 85

U

URLs, handling unvalidated redirects, 147

User identity, OWASP Cloud top 10 risks, 148

Usernames

authentication examples, 55–56

hacking, 53

insecure coding practices, 179

securing logins, 51

sending over SSL, 99

user behavior and, 84–85

V

Verification, "trust but verify" approach, 160

Verisign, sources of SSL certificates, 104

Virtual machines. *See* VMs (virtual machines)

Virus protection, OWASP Web Services Cheat Sheet, 134

VMs (virtual machines)

ART (Android Runtime), 7

DVM (Dalvik Virtual Machine), 1

securing Android in future and, 190

VMware Air Watch MDM solution, 177–178

Vulnerabilities, OWASP Top 10 risks, 147

W

Wearables, 186–187

Weather Underground

Charles Proxy test of security of network traffic, 103–107

HTTP/HTTPS calls to, 88–91, 98

Web, session management, 82–84

Web browsers, session management, 82–84

Web servers

HIPAA compliance, 149–150

weak server-side control, 14–15

Web Service Description Language (WSDL), 132

Web services, 131

asymmetric key encryption of API keys, 94–99

cross-platform apps and, 135–140

hiding encryption keys in, 127

HIPAA compliance and, 149–150

overview of, 131–132

OWASP Cloud Top 10 risks, 148–149

OWASP Top 10 risks, 146–147

OWASP Web Services Cheat Sheet, 133–134

protecting API keys, 88–92, 131

replay attacks, 135

SQL injection attacks, 142–144

WebView attacks, 140–142

XSS (Cross Site Scripting) issues, 145–146

Websites, hacking, 131

WebView attacks

overview of, 140–142

SQL injection attacks, 142–144

XSS (Cross Site Scripting) issues, 145–146

Wiping devices, 168

WSDL (Web Service Description Language), 132

X

XSD, validation of soap messages, 133

XSS (Cross-Site Scripting)

OWASP Top 10 risks, 146

OWASP Web Services Cheat Sheet, 134

WebView attacks, 142, 145–146

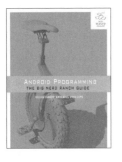

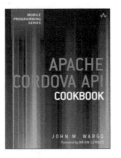